SKIP PROBATE

DUMP YOUR LAWYER
Create Your OWN Living Trust

SAVE YOUR ESTATE
$THOUSANDS$

Sam Hauck

SKIP
PROBATE

Dump Your Lawyer
Create Your OWN Living Trust

A guide on how to skip probate written by a nonlawyer with
the truth about probate and lawyers and how to avoid both.

Copyright © 2018 by Sam Hauck.

COVER AND INTERIOR DESIGNED BY
Shadow Canyon Graphics
La Veta, Colorado

ISBN-13: 978-1723383854
ISBN-10: 1723383856

First Edition
10 9 8 7 6 5 4 3 2 1

PRINTED IN THE UNITED STATES OF AMERICA

CONTENTS

INTRODUCTION

The phone rang. It was a lawyer. My father died three days ago and already a lawyer was calling. He had my father's will and I was named the executor. He said the will must be presented for probate. He explained that probate is a legal matter that everyone experiences. (That's not true, of course, but he said it anyway).

The lawyer suggested I meet him in his office. I did. He had papers for me to sign permitting him to do the probate. Most executors sign. I did not. I told him I would do the probate myself. I watched his jaw drop. He just lost $25,000. He gave me the will and I left.

Probate is the legal process of verifying the legality of a Last Will and Testament. The Probate Court makes the decision to accept or reject the will. The Court then oversees the settlement of the estate and distribution of assets to the beneficiaries.

Probate could take a year or more, and the cost can be excessive. A probate cost in excess of five percent of the estate is common. This is money that would be better given to the children or grandchildren.

As executor I took my father's estate through probate and satisfied the demands of the Court. It was not fun. The experience encouraged me to probate-proof the rest of the family estates and inspired me to write this book to help others probate-proof theirs.

The best way to avoid probate is create a revocable living trust. Many of us are unfamiliar with the living trust. We think an attorney must prepare it. Your family attorney may suggest you don't need a trust because your estate is too small. That is bad advice. The small estate needs a living trust too. The attorney may suggest the cost of creating a trust will be more than probate will cost later. This is also bad advice. Those who fail to create a living trust experience the excessive cost, delay, and aggravation of probate.

You can create your living trust in the privacy of your home using readily available software for your computer, and you should. Almost everyone should have a trust. The trust is the bests place for some assets, and it serves as a pay-on-death beneficiary for many others.

Do it yourself? Isn't that risky? Your family lawyer—in fact most lawyers—will say you can get into trouble doing it yourself. No you won't. The trust you create will be professional and legal now and for-ever no matter where you live or resettle. What's more, the trust will remain private. The government will never see it unless someone sues the trust or its grantor, and that is very rare.

This book is different than all other books on wills, trusts and pro-bate avoidance. The reason—the author is not an attorney. I cannot write in complicated and difficult-to-read legalese. I have never been trained for that. Sorry, but you will have to accept simple English.

Also, the fact that the author is not an attorney is an absolute pos-itive. I give you the straight truth about probate without the risk of being accused of ethical malpractice or professional heresy.

The suggestions and recommendations made throughout this book are the result of helping family and friends successfully avoid probate. They have been proven valid through experience. They are not legal advice. If you want legal advice, contact an attorney.

Probate proof your estate. Create your own living trust. Your fami-ly will be forever grateful. And no lawyer will call, ever.

DISCLAIMER

This book is written from the perspective of a layperson, with real world experience in the probate process. The author is not a lawyer—that is the whole point of the book. The author does not practice law. Those readers requiring and looking for legal advice should see a law-yer. If you don't know whether you need a lawyer or not—then you should ask a lawyer. Neither the author nor the publisher is responsible for any damages you might incur in relying on the contents of this book. The content of this book is solely the opinion of the author. You have paid for a book of ideas, not a law degree. Whether you use these concepts or not is entirely your judgment and discretion.

Chapter One

WHAT IS PROBATE?

Probate: The process of establishing the validity of a will before a judicial authority.

PROBATE IS THE PROCESS OF PROVING, before a court of law, the validity of a deceased person's Last Will and Testament. If that was the only concern no one in the family would mind. But, in addition, and in accordance with state law, the court supervises the settlement of the estate and the transfer of property to the beneficiaries named in the will. If you die intestate (there is no will), the state decides by law who gets what. The property usually goes to the next of kin, but there is no guarantee. The Court's decision may not please everybody.

A state court administers probate at the courthouse in the county where you had legal residence (and not necessarily where you died). The name of the court varies. In some states it is called the Surrogate's Court, in others the Chancery Court, or Orphans' Court. Actually, in many states the Circuit Court or District Court has jurisdiction over probate matters. Amazingly, in almost a third of the states the court with probate jurisdiction is actually called the Probate Court.

The Federal government is not involved. Well, yes it is—the IRS anxiously awaits the taxes they hope to collect. Good estate planning can reduce taxes. Recommendations made in this book on how to reduce or eliminate taxes can easily be made part of your estate plan. (See Chapter 14).

If you spend time in more than one state, the Court will decide residence based on where you voted, worked, registered your car, had friends, etc. If you have property in more than one state, ancillary probate of that property can occur in that state too. Probate in more than one state is definitely a burden to avoid. That's only one of many reasons to avoid probate.

Probate laws differ slightly in each state, but the primary goal is to insure that the wishes of the decedent are carried out to the letter. During settlement of the probate estate, the Court oversees the activities of the executor until the government is fully satisfied.

Probate can be a terrible experience for the family. Privacy is lost—probate cases are open to the public. If the deceased was a public figure or of questionable character, this could be embarrassing for the family.

Probate costs too much, not only the probate fee, but attorney's fees too. Unfortunately, these costs are paid for with money that would otherwise go to the heirs.

Probate takes too long. If an attorney is hired to take the estate through probate, the family may not understand what is going on or why the case is taking so long. The family may feel it has lost control. They ask, "when in the world will this case end?" I recommend you eliminate all of these aggravations by avoiding probate. Yes indeed, skip probate.

When is Probate Necessary?

Probate is necessary when a deceased person's property cannot pass automatically to a designated beneficiary or next of kin. Assets held in joint ownership go to the surviving joint owner. When a beneficiary is designated to receive an asset when the owner dies, that asset passes to the beneficiary free of probate. Assets held in a living trust pass without probate to the beneficiary listed in the trust. These are the best three ways to avoid probate. They are discussed in detail in chapters five, six, and seven.

The Probate Process

The process starts by submitting a petition to the court to probate the Last Will and Testament of the deceased. The court will determine if the testator, the person who wrote the will, was competent and if he or she signed willingly. The court must also decide if this is the most recent will. The court honors only the most recent will.

To accomplish this the court may decide to hold a hearing. Notice must be given, usually by mail, to everyone mentioned in the will and to the legal next of kin. When notice is completed the court sets a date to admit the will for probate. A will may be contested when there appears to be undue influence on the decedent when he made the will. Someone may claim the will is a fraud, or question the mental competency of the signer, or the conditions under which it was signed. A relative may feel he or she was wrongfully cut out.

Objections are heard in open court and thus made public. The press could be there. It could be an entertaining day at the courthouse.

If there are no objections, the court will accept the will and appoint an executor. The person(s) chosen as executor(s) are usually the same person or persons named as executors in the will (if you have one, and almost half of us do not) to act as the personal representative of the deceased. If the executor meets the qualifications set forth in state statutes, and the court deems him or her competent, the court then issues a document called Letters Testamentary (or a Letter of Administration in the event the deceased died without a will). This document authorizes the executor or administrator to settle the estate.

In most cases Letters Testamentary or Letters of Administration can be issued without the formal hearing mentioned above, but that is not guaranteed.

When all the distributions have been made to the beneficiaries, the taxes have been paid, and the reports filed with the court, a release is given to the executors and the estate is closed.

It sound like fun, doesn't it? Trying to satisfy the court could be a full time job.

Probate Procedures

Procedures differ from state to state, but this is a general outline of the procedures which may be necessary when settling an estate under probate.

1. Obtain from the court with probate jurisdiction the proper petition or application forms that are required when filing for probate. Family members may do this but more commonly an attorney does this for the family.

2. File the petition with the probate judge asking that the will be admitted for probate. Also present the original will and a death certificate. If there is no will, state that the deceased died without a will. Recommend person(s) to act as executor(s) or administrator(s) of the estate.

3. Pay the probate fee to the court.

4. Provide notice to the legal next of kin and everyone mentioned in the will.

5. The court may set a date to admit the will for probate.

6. If the will is accepted for probate and approved, and the executor meets the state requirements, the court will issue Letters Testamentary or a Letter of Administration permitting the executor to act on behalf of the estate.

7. The executor may be required to post a surety bond unless the will states that the executor shall serve without bond.

8. A death notice must be published in the local newspaper (usually more than once) seeking creditors who may file claims against the estate.

9. An inventory of assets must be prepared and filed with the court. Appraisals may be required to obtain current values.

10. A fee or tax may be payable to the court. The amount may depend on the value of the estate.

11. The executor opens an estate checking account at a bank after presenting Letters Testamentary or a Letters of Administration.

12. The executor collects all assets.

13. The executor pays all the debts of the descendent and the expenses of estate administration.

14. Tax returns are filed for the estate and taxes paid.

15. Assets are distributed to the beneficiaries or heirs.

16. An accounting of the estate assets and expenses must be filed and approved by the probate court.

17. On petition the probate court will close the administration of the estate and provide a release.

I have listed 17 procedures for settling an estate under probate court supervision. There could be more. If you would like to subject you executor to these 17 (or more), then do nothing to avoid probate.

Please realize that when you avoid probate you will simplify matters for everyone, not only for your executor but also everyone in the family.

Skip Probate

If you are able to skip probate—because you have a non-probate estate—there are only five procedures typically necessary. These five are:

1. Open an estate checking account
2. Collect the assets
3. Pay the debts and expenses
4. Pay the taxes
5. Distribute the assets to the beneficiaries and heirs.

Probate proceedings in some states are abbreviated and simple, and the court may exercise very little supervision. In others states the requirements may be extensive and aggravating. Even if proceedings are simple in your state, skip probate anyway. Your family will be glad you did.

Probate was a great idea. It was designed to protect orphans and widows and prevent confiscation of property which rightfully belonged to the innocent survivors of the deceased. But probate is of no benefit to most families. It can be a huge aggravation. Small wonder probate avoidance has become so popular.

Many lawyers claim that probate is not a big deal. Of course it's not a big deal for lawyers. They make a ton of money taking death estates through probate.

Many people consider probate avoidance a mandatory goal, and they should. It's easier than you think and you can do it yourself.

CHAPTER TWO

AVOID PROBATE

EVERYONE HAS HEARD HOW families have suffered under the invasive and costly process known as probate. Every experienced executor knows how aggravating it was to deal with the requirements of the probate court. They all agree that it would have been better if probate could have been avoided and the estate could have been settled privately.

Here are some of the situations an executor may experience while trying to settle an estate under probate:

Aggravation

A trip to the courthouse is never fun, whether it's to pay a fine, report for jury duty, or any reason. In fact, a visit to the probate court can be very discouraging. How often have you gone to the courthouse and successfully completed new business on the first visit?

After your executor finds the right court, and this can be difficult and time consuming in a large and populous county, he may not feel very welcome. He can't expect to get a lot of help from the probate court staff.

I have personal experience. I went to the courthouse to see how difficult it was to file a will for probate. This was a test. I asked the clerk for the petition form to start the probate process. The clerk answered, "We don't have forms you can use. We accept the forms the attorneys submit." After I asked more questions the clerk suggested, "the only place you can get forms is from the State Bar Association." A call to the state bar revealed they don't give away forms. It fact, they don't sell them either. The state bar's answer was, "we supply the forms only to our member attorneys." So much for friendly help.

Some probate court staff can be very helpful. But others fail to give you the time of day unless you are an attorney. Some clerks' attitude seem to be, "Go to the law library and figure it out for yourself." It is distressing when you realize our taxes pay these people's salaries. You certainly don't want to put your executor through treatment like this. Plan to avoid probate of your estate.

Cost

Your executor may do the probate of your will and settle your estate without hiring a lawyer. Unfortunately, he may not realize this unless you explain and discuss this with him beforehand, or he reads this book. Both would be advisable.

Suppose your executor decides to settle the estate himself. After he finds the right court, and is successful in presenting your will for probate, your estate can expect to be charged a filing fee. The fee is at least $35 even for the smallest estates. When states charge a flat fee for everyone, the small estate pays a higher percentage of the estate in fees than does the larger estate. That's not fair to the small estate, but complaints won't help. State law is not likely to change.

Filing costs may be extreme. In New York, for example, estates larger than $500,000 pay $1,000. This is an outrageous waste of money.

I believe that every time you pay a fee to the government you are paying a fine or a tax. The probate-filing fee is another tax. Your estate will receive nothing in return for this tax.

If your executor hires a lawyer to do the probate, costs go way up. Lawyers are happy to write wills for their clients for the typical hourly fee. Then some lawyers recommend that the original be stored in their law office safe. They have a plan. The lawyer anticipates a handsome fee in the future when the will goes to probate. You have heard the expression, "possession is 90 percent of ownership." When your lawyer retains possession of your original will—it's the original that is present-ed for probate—he has the inside track to a handsome income later.

Probate is a huge source of profit for lawyers. This is easy money for the lawyer for very little work. In fact, a lot of the work is farmed out to paralegals. Without question, the fee charged by the attorney doing the probate takes the biggest bite out of the estate.

Costs vary from state to state, but most often the attorney's fee is expressed as a percentage of the gross estate. If it were based on a per-centage of the net estate, which would be more sensible, the cost might be significantly less.

A probate attorney fee of five percent of the value of the gross estate is common. It may be more if the attorney is permitted by state statute to charge more. There may also be hourly fees if extra work is required. It is not unusual for a small estate to be charged more on a percentage basis than a large estate. Don't be surprised when a small estate of $15,000 net worth pays $1000. AARP claims that cost to settle an estate through probate can eat up as much as 10 percent of the estate.

The lawyer may wish to charge a percentage fee based on the size of the estate. Some may offer a flat fee. Or he may offer to do the pro-bate charging an hourly fee. I feel this is a scary open-ended contract. I would shy away from that. In any event, fees are always negotiable and are always more than it would cost your estate if the executor did the probate herself.

Consider this double cost. When a spouse dies, some or all of his or her assets, not held in joint tenancy, may have to pass to the surviving spouse through probate. There will be probate fees and court costs. When the second spouse dies, there will be another probate. On the second probate many of the same assets that passed to the surviving spouse as a result of the first probate will be subjected to probate fees and court costs a second time.

There is no way to justify the cost of probate. It does absolutely nothing for the family. This is money which otherwise would have gone to the beneficiaries. Unless there is a foreseen complication or conflict, there is no need to go to court.

The probate system is sustained by the state legislatures and by lawyers who run the courts and belong to the State Bar Associations and cherish the system. As a result the probate system is not likely to change.

I mentioned the high cost of probate to my good friend, the retired dean of a prestigious law school. He agreed attorney fees for probate were too high. He told me about a meeting he attended with members of the State Bar. He did not say when that occurred or who was present, and I didn't ask. When he suggested at that meeting that attorneys charge their hourly attorney rate only for the work they actually perform, and a lesser rate lesser rate for that done buy paralegals and office staff, he met immediate resistance. He said that greatly upset him.

He was a fair and honest man. My friend passed away recently. Some attorneys continue to overcharge for probate work.

Time

Everyone knows that probate takes time. A year is not unusual. It could take two years or more, and nobody knows why or whether that time is justified.

Preparation of the petition is time consuming. The petition may be lengthy and involved. It might require a list with location of all the assets and their value. The clerk may reject the petition or other court filings if they fail to meet the court's requirements. When the filing is eventually successful, a date may be set in the future to hear the petition. The judge, executor, and the lawyers must all be present on that date. This may cause delay.

Your executor can settle the estate himself, and he can proceed quickly. It may be a tedious job, but will save the estate considerable money.

But if your executor decides to hire a lawyer to do the probate, he should pick a good one. Good lawyers are busy and expensive. If a good lawyer is hired, he will have many projects in play. Don't expect him to work full time on your case. His fee is probably fixed and already guaranteed. If other projects pop up, they will probably take precedence over yours.

There are other factors that can delay the case. If the probate is settled quickly, the case will appear to have been too easy. Then the executor and the beneficiaries may question if the attorney's fee was justified. Perhaps the attorney made a bundle of money this year and would prefer to delay completion of your case until next year and thus defer the income and taxes until next year. You will never know.

Some attorneys routinely turn probate cases over to paralegals. This may speed the case considerably, but there is no guarantee that when he gets it back from the paralegal he will proceed to a prompt conclusion. The simple fact is, he will get to it when he gets to it.

Maybe I've been too harsh on lawyers here. But one thing is certain. An estate which avoids lawyers and skips probate can be settled quickly.

Privacy

What you own is nobody's business, not your neighbor's, not your friend's, and certainly not the government's. In fact, your children and other family members don't need to know either. It's all private.

When you die, and your will is filed for probate with the state government—the probate court—it becomes a public document. All privacy is lost. Everything about your estate and your wealth becomes public information: what you were worth, how much you owed and to whom, how much or how little you left to charity, who your beneficiaries are, which of your children you left out of your will, and how much you gave to each beneficiary.

In most cases your will gets filed for probate and nobody cares because your will is one of many being presented to the court. But if you were a strange character, a famous person, or a leader in your community, someone may be interested. The news media may take a look. They will do anything for a story. The resulting news could be scandalous, or at lease embarrassing to your beneficiaries.

The Last Will and Testaments of Richard Nixon, Elvis Presley, and Jacqueline Kennedy Onassis are available on the internet. So much for privacy. Yours probably won't make the internet, but why take the chance that some nosey reporter or former business adversary may decide to take advantage of you? Skip probate.

The Not-So-Private Advertisement for Creditors

During settlement of an estate under probate the executor is usually required by law to advertise in the local newspaper (perhaps twice or more) for anyone to whom the estate may be indebted to come forward and submit a claim. The ad usually appears as a "notice" in the classified section of the newspaper. The probate court should provide the executor with the requirements for these ads and the specific format. Usually the ads are small and insignificant. But there is no reason they can't be larger. A recent ad in a Wyoming small town newspaper was two columns wide and six inches long.

Frankly, these ads are an embarrassment to the family. In most cases they are unnecessary. In many cases they serve only as an advertisement for the attorneys, paid for by the estate of the deceased. It makes the attorneys appear important. And it should make you wish once again that the estate had avoided probate

Loss of Control

When an attorney is hired to file the will for settle the estate, it is common for the family to feel abandoned. They may not understand what the attorney is doing or if any progress is being made.

Under probate, the beneficiaries normally get nothing until the case is completed. The judge will have to approve any request for funds for beneficiaries with immediate needs such as medical expenses or tuition to start college. And even so, the amount may not be enough to meet future needs. Imagine the embarrassment of having to ask a judge for money that is rightfully yours anyway.

If communications fail between the family and the attorney, and the family is not sufficiently advised as to what progress is being made, what recourse does the family have? Can the executor fire the attorney? Suppose he refuses to be fired? After all, he is probably under contract. Does the family hire another lawyer to help fire the first one? Or does the executor go to the probate judge for help? Remember, the judge is a lawyer too. Good luck.

Double Probate

If you haven't taken action to avoid probate where you live, it is likely that you haven't taken action to avoid probate of property, such as a vacation home or condo, in another state. The result can be probate in two states; probate in the state where you lived, and ancillary probate in the second state. Imagine two probate courts, two probate judges, and probably a local lawyer in the second state. The probability of probate in two states doubles the need to skip probate completely.

WHEN MIGHT PROBATE BE ACCEPTABLE?

There may be instances in which probate might be acceptable. For example, if your estate has a negative net worth as a result of large unpaid bills or a lawsuit judgment against it, your beneficiaries may stand to get nothing. In this case why go to the trouble of avoiding probate? In fact, your executor might ultimately decide to decline appointment as executor, because this could be an unpleasant estate settlement incurring the wrath of creditors, particularly when they discover they may not get the full amount they believe is due them. On the other hand, she may wish to remain as executor because, even though she may have been designated as a beneficiary, the executor's fee may be all she will get from the estate. The attorney can advise what estate settlement tasks she should perform and the amount she will be permitted to charge.

The attorney hired to do the probate and settle a low value estate will charge the maximum fee allowed by state law and get paid first. Estate settlement costs and all taxes due will be paid before any creditors get anything. The probate judge will decide how the residue is distributed among the creditors. When the probate case is closed and a release is provided by the probate court, your executor and the attorney become protected from liability.

Some people—for whatever reason—don't want a family member or independent trustee running things. Or they don't have family members to appoint as executor or successor trustee. They would rather hire an attorney to take the estate through probate. The other option: create a trust to probate-proof the estate, and have an attorney settle the trust. That would eliminate probate court costs.

If you are convinced you want to skip probate, read the rest of this book and get started. Probate avoidance is worth the effort.

— Chapter Three —

UNDERSTANDING YOUR ESTATE

You don't have to be a wealthy landowner with an opulent mansion and a stable full of racehorses to own an estate. All of us, either rich or poor, have an estate. Your estate is simply the value of all the property you own. It consists of all sorts of assets. These include personal property, both tangible and intangible, and real property. And maybe some "unreal" property too! Everyone has some weird stuff, but that's okay.

You and your executor, and the successor trustee of any trust you may have, should know everything about your estate and the assets you own. This knowledge is necessary so you can probate-proof your assets now, and the executor and successor trustee can easily settle your estate when you are gone.

The Gross Estate

A person's gross estate encompasses all the property, personal and real, owned by an individual before any deductions for debts, taxes, funeral expenses, attorney's fees, and administrative costs are deducted.

To avoid probate of your estate all of your assets must be probate-proof. Let's look at personal property first.

Personal property is all the property you own other than land, buildings, or other improvements to the land. This personal property is either tangible or intangible.

Tangible personal property is that property which you can touch. It includes:

Animals	Clothing
Antiques	Precious Metals
Art	Hobby Collections
Books	Tools
Furniture	Farm Equipment
Kitchenware	Vehicles
Jewelry	

Tangible personal property can usually be passed to your named beneficiaries or heirs, given away, trashed, or disposed of by your executor through private sale or public auction. No probate avoidance planning is required for this property because most of the assets have no ownership documents and thus no accounting. The exception, of course, is vehicles, which are tangible personal property for which there are title or registration documents. Nonetheless, transfer to a new owner is very easy. (See chapter 16 for probate avoidance procedures for vehicles)

Intangible personal property is property you cannot touch. It is property for which you hold paper reflecting its value. Examples are:

Stocks	Promissory Notes
Bonds	Mortgages
Brokerage Accounts	Insurance Policies
Bank Accounts	Royalties
Certificates of Deposit	Patents
Retirement Accounts	Copyrights
Trust Agreements	Business Interests
Private Investment	Businesses

Intangible personal property requires a probate avoidance procedure to remain free from probate. The three best ways are joint ownership, a pay-on-death beneficiary designation on the asset's registration document, or holding the asset in a trust. These methods are discussed in the next chapter. (For probate avoidance procedures for each specific asset see Chapter 16).

Real property includes all types of real estate:

> Your Home
> Your Vacation Home
> Your Condo in Hawaii
> Commercial Real Estate
> Farms and Ranches
> Unimproved Land

A note here about real estate: Real estate is something you can touch (tangible personal property). But real estate is also something for which you also hold paper, a deed. So that also makes it intangible property. Right? Nope, real estate is neither tangible nor intangible. It's real property. That may not make much sense. And I can't explain it.

The living trust is the most common—and best—way to hold real estate to avoid probate. (See Chapter 16).

The Net Estate

Your net estate is the value of your gross estate minus your liabilities such as mortgages, loans, and other debts. Your net estate is equal to your net worth. After your death the value of your net estate is reduced by funeral costs and the costs of settling the estate.

It's a good idea to determine the value of your net estate from time to time. You may have done so when you applied for a home loan or equity line of credit. You listed your assets in the column on the left side of the loan application, and your liabilities in the right column. At the bottom you subtracted the liabilities from the assets and the answer was your net worth. That is the value of your net estate. Of course your net estate changes continuously. Hopefully it increases in value each time you make the calculation.

The Probate Estate

All estate property that cannot go directly to the beneficiaries after your death must go through probate. This property is known as Probate Property. The existence of probate property results in a Probate Estate after your death. When attorneys, bankers, or estate planners tell you "that asset will flow into the estate," they are talking about the probate estate. For example, the proceeds from the sale of the deceased's home, unless the home was held in a trust or in joint ownership, will "flow" into the probate estate and pass from your will through probate to the next owner. If you want to avoid probate you must make sure that, first, you do not have probate property in your gross estate and second, that some otherwise innocuous asset won't "pay into your estate" and create a probate estate for you after your death. Now is the time to fix it, and convert your potential probate estate into a non-probate estate. It is not difficult. You can do it easily yourself.

Establish a non-probate estate. Employ the probate avoidance methods described in the next chapter.

The Non-Probate Estate

The non-probate estate is comprised of assets that do not have to go through probate. As I mentioned earlier, these are assets that are held in joint ownership whereby the survivor retains the asset, and assets for which there is a designated beneficiary, and assets held in a trust. And of course, all non-probate estates have tangible personal property that can be sold, given away, or thrown away.

To avoid probate, you must create a non-probate estate. After your death, when your executor is asked why she hasn't filed your will for probate, she can respond with the best of all answers, "this was a non-probate estate." The word "was" is significant. When you have a non-probate estate while you live, after your death there will no longer be an estate. All your assets will now belong to your beneficiaries. That was your intention. These assets may not get transferred to the beneficiaries immediately, but the executor and successor trustee will do that as soon as practicable. Since this was a non-probate estate, there was no need to file the will for probate and no need for the executor/trustee to go anywhere near the courthouse.

What about tangible personal property intentionally left in your will? Those assets go to the beneficiaries named in the will, or pour over into your living trust if you made a pour-over will. (See Chapter 12 concerning the pour-over will).

It's an either/or situation. Either you have a non-probate estate while you live or a probate estate after your death. The choice is simple. You need a non-probate estate now.

The Life Estate

Since we have been discussing estates, here is another estate that may be of interest to you. The life estate could be useful in estate planning.

The life estate is defined as the right to use or occupy real property for the duration of one's life. Usually someone grants this right to a person (usually a family member) by deed or as a gift in a will. The duration of the life estate is measured by the life of that person.

George wants to provide for his older brother, Earl. George creates a Life Estate Trust that grants Earl the right to live in or receive the rent from a home for the rest of Earl's life. Earl, the beneficiary, has the right to use the property, or to receive rent from its use, but never becomes legal owner of the property. When Earl dies, the property passes to George's daughter, Susan.

The document could read something like this: "I grant to my brother, Earl Stone, the right to live in, or receive rent from, my house at 3435 Spencer Street, (my city), (my state), until his death," or "I give to my daughter, Susan Stevens, the real property located at 3435 Spencer Street, (my city), (my state), subject to a life estate to my brother, Earl." This means that Earl gets to live or receive rent from the property until he dies, then Susan inherits the property.

If the life estate document is structured properly, the asset will avoid probate. The Life Estate Trust can do that. But if the property, instead of being granted in a Life Estate Trust is granted under a will, probate is likely. Property which passes to the final beneficiary through a will rather than through a trust usually has to go through probate.

A life estate is a thoughtful gift to a relative or friend. If you want to create a life estate, seek the help of an attorney.

Chapter Four

HOW TO AVOID PROBATE

The Three Ways to Avoid Probate

THERE ARE A CONFUSING number of ways to avoid probate. I prefer the most important three ways. They are:

1. Hold the assets in **joint ownership** (with right of survivorship).
2. **Designate a beneficiary** to receive the asset upon your death.
3. Hold the assets in your **living trust**.

The three ways are commonly referred to as **will substitutes** because they remove from your will assets which would otherwise be subject to probate. The will substitutes are simple, easy to understand, and cost little or nothing to create. None require help from a lawyer. If you use these will substitutes, you can create a non-probate estate. After your death all property will pass directly to your heirs or beneficiaries. There will be no probate. There will be no lawyers, and no probate courts will have oversight. Your executor and successor trustee will simply settle your estate and trust privately. Let's look at the three ways.

Joint Ownership

Joint ownership is the most common form of probate avoidance. Married couples and many unmarried partners use it. Joint ownership is very easy to establish. Simply fill in the owners' names on some simple paperwork, and it's done. Later the deceased owner's share passes automatically by law to the surviving owner, or owners, without probate, provided you have selected the joint ownership method that allows such transfer. Joint ownership is discussed in Chapter 5.

Designate a Beneficiary to Receive Your Assets

Designation is the legal term for naming a beneficiary to receive your assets upon your death. When you open an account, buy a certificate of deposit, buy life insurance, open an IRA, or engage in a host or other transactions, it is customary and essential to name a beneficiary to receive the asset when you die. This is known as a pay-on-death (P.O.D.) designation.

Designating a beneficiary is easy to do. Simply place the name of the beneficiary on the registration document. All custodians have forms available for this purpose. Upon your death the beneficiary identifies herself to the custodian of the asset and provides a death certificate of the deceased. The asset will be promptly paid or transferred to the beneficiary free of probate. The designation of beneficiary method of probate avoidance is further addressed in Chapter 6.

Hold the Assets in Your Living Trust

The living trust is a trust document you create while you are alive. You live and the trust lives. You transfer property to the trust, and as trustee you control that property. Upon your death the successor trustee transfers the property held in trust to the final beneficiaries free of probate. The living trust is explained in Chapter 7.

The Supposed Other Ways To Avoid Probate

I prefer the three basic ways to avoid probate: joint ownership, pay–on-death beneficiary, and the living trust.

Some authors list additional ways. Eight possible ways are commonly suggested, sometimes more. It makes you wonder if there are just eight, or maybe really 10 ways, or perhaps more.

The other supposed ways are usually variations of the basic three or are ways that avoid probate for a select few items in some states. If some of these are available in your state, you could consider using them if they don't create more work for your executor and successor trustee after your death. Let's look at some of these "additional" ways:

1. Transfer-on-death (T.O.D.) designation is permitted for brokerage accounts, stocks, and bonds. You designate someone, or perhaps a trust, as T.O.D. beneficiary. Upon your death the account is transferred to the beneficiary. This is not a different scheme. It is merely a pay-on-death with a new name. It's one of the basic three.

2. Name a T.O.D. beneficiary for your vehicles. In a few states you can name a beneficiary to receive your car or truck. Since it is available to just a few of us, those few for whom it is available might consider it a separate method, but of course it's the basic pay-on-death renamed.

3. Some states have a non-probate transfer procedure for vehicles by affidavit. Again, that is available for only a few of us. It is nice to know if it is available in your state, but probably not something you should plan in advance to use. (See Chapter 16 for procedures on how to keep you vehicles out of probate).

4. Buy Life Insurance. The money you spend to pay the premium for life insurance will never go through probate. It is gone forever. Life insurance is purchased to take care of your loved ones after you die. Or life insurance is pur-

chased to provide money for your heirs so they can pay inheritance taxes without selling the ranch. Sometimes life insurance is purchased on your business partner's life so you can purchase his half of the business after his death. These are estate-planning strategies and are not done primarily to avoid probate.

5. Give it away. Many estate planners mention gift giving as a method of avoiding probate. It is a no-brainer that if you give it away it is no longer yours and it won't ever have to go through probate. If you die penniless, you will never have to worry about probate. But most giving is done to avoid taxes. Whether you give money or property to charity now or establish a charitable remainder trust so the charity gets the money when you die, you do it primarily to reduce income taxes now or estate inheritance taxes later. Yes, the assets you give away avoid probate.

6. Small estate procedures; There are generally two ways to administer the inheritance of small estates without going through a full-fledged probate.

   a. The first is by **affidavit**. Upon the death of the owner, the beneficiary listed in the will fills out a claim form. When the institution holding the property—a bank, for example—receives the affidavit and a copy of the death certificate of the deceased, it releases the property or the money. The affidavit claim can usually be done without the help of a lawyer.

   b. The other method is **summary administration** whereby a judge opens the estate and immediately distributes the assets to the beneficiaries. This might also be referred to as simplified probate. This might be what your family lawyer was referring to when he suggested that you don't need a living trust because probate procedures are very simple in your state. Rubbish. Probate procedures are never simple enough. And this method at the very least requires a trip to the courthouse. A trip that probate avoidance eliminates. Why go to the courthouse if you don't have to?

Most states have one or the other of these procedures. A few states have procedures that are a variation of the two methods. To find out if your state has small estate procedures, use your favorite search engine and search "(your state) small estate procedures" or simply "small estate procedures." You will quickly find specifics about your state. The maximum value allowed to qualify as a small estate usually means the maximum value of the probate assets left in your will, i.e., those assets which have to go through probate before the asset can be given to the heirs.

Are the small estate procedures a primary way to avoid probate, and should you plan your estate with the expectation that your executor will use them during the settlement of your estate? No! They have too many limitations, and in many cases they require approval of the probate judge.

What If You Hold Some Assets In Your Will?

Assets left in you will are generally considered probate assets. However, your **tangible** personal property—those items you can touch—namely the household goods, coin collections, porch furniture, garden tools, and usually everything else in your home or on the farm can be sold at auction, or sold privately, or given away. There will be no probate for this tangible personal property.

If you leave in your will **intangible** personal property—the property you hold paper to such as bank accounts, brokerage accounts, CDs, cars and trucks—it will **not** avoid probate. This property will have to go through probate on its way to those you want to receive it.

Likewise, **real property** must not be left in your will. Hold real estate in you living trust. The living trust is the best way to keep real estate out of probate.

If you read somewhere, or someone told you, that if you have a will your estate is guaranteed to go through probate, forget it. That is the common mantra of the guy who wants to provide you with a living trust, for a big fee. The mere possession of a will does not guarantee probate. In fact, you need a will. That is where you can state who gets the tangible personal property you intentionally left in your will. And it's where you name guardians for your minor children. (See Chapter 12, The Will).

CHAPTER FIVE

JOINT OWNERSHIP

The First of the Three Ways
To Avoid Probate

JOINT OWNERSHIP IS THE most frequently used of the three ways to avoid probate. Married couples usually select some form of joint ownership for their bank accounts, brokerage accounts, their car, and their home. Many unmarried couples use it as well. Everyone knows that after the first owner dies, the surviving owner gets the account. It is such a common practice that we set up joint ownership automatically. Some people don't realize joint ownership is a probate avoidance tool, but that is an automatic benefit.

Many couples wrongly believe that holding assets in joint ownership will avoid probate and that is all the estate planning they need. You may have heard a friend say, "Oh, we have all our assets in joint names, so we're all set." Well, they're not. Joint ownership is not a panacea. There are advantages to joint ownership, but there are serious disadvantages too.

Some types of joint ownership methods avoid probate and others do not. When one owner dies the survivor may or may not inherit the deceased owner's share, depending on the type of ownership. The deceased owner's share may become a probate asset. If joint owners suffer simultaneous deaths, there could be two probate estates for the heirs to settle. In this chapter I will identify the serious disadvantage associated with joint ownership and suggest remedies.

JOINT OWNERSHIP THAT AVOIDS PROBATE

Joint Tenancy with the Right of Survivorship (JTWROS)

Joint ownership with the right of survivorship is the most common form of joint ownership. It is offered in all 50 states and the District of Columbia, but there are limitations in Alaska and Texas. In Alaska there is joint tenancy in real estate only for husband and wife, who may own as tenants by the entirety. (See Tenants by the Entirety below). In Texas a separate written agreement must be filled out and signed. All financial institutions in Texas have these forms and can walk you through the procedure.

Joint tenancy is easy to establish and costs nothing. The owners of the asset are known as joint tenants (although they don't have to rent anything). They don't have to be married. Two sisters will do, or a brother and sister, or three siblings, or a paperboy and his mom. They don't have to be related either. Obviously sex doesn't't matter, and neither does sexual orientation. Anyone can establish a joint ownership.

In the overwhelming number of cases joint tenancy involves two tenants, but there can be three or more. An example is the Convenience Checking Account (See Chapter 13).

To insure that joint tenancy is guaranteed, the words "joint tenancy with the right of survivorship" or the initials "JTWROS" must be spelled out on the registration document. Make sure the document when completed includes these designations or the right of survivorship terminology that is accepted in your state. When the first joint owner dies, the survivor automatically, after completion of some simple paperwork, owns the deceased's share and becomes sole owner of the property. No action is immediately necessary. It's still the survivor's property now and into the future. Check with the financial institution on the need for immediate action to transfer the account to the survivor as sole owner, and with your attorney on the need to create a new deed for real estate. Very likely no action needs to be taken. I am aware of a widow who kept her home in joint names with her deceased husband for 30 year after his death. When she ultimately sold her home the new deed to the buyer merely mentioned that the husband died in 1978.

Here is something to consider. A joint owner can break the tenancy at any time by transferring his or her share. This is not common, of course, but it is possible. It is of little concern to most couples. If one tenant were to sell his share of the joint tenancy property to someone else, then the owners are no longer joint tenants but tenants in common. For example: Bill and Ed own a house together as joint tenants. Ed decides he wants to leave his half of the house to his daughter, Eleanor. So he creates a quitclaim deed transferring his half share of the house to himself as a tenant in common, and he records the deed at the register of deeds office in his county court house. In his will he names Eleanor as the death beneficiary of the house. When Ed dies Bill does not get the house. Eleanor gets Ed's half, so Bill and Eleanor now own the house as tenants in common. That is an awkward arrangement.

If you are concerned that your joint owner might transfer away his portion of an asset which would become yours upon his death, then consider tenancy by the entirety.

Tenancy by the Entirety

Tenancy by the entirety is for married couples only. It is very much like joint tenancy but has some advantages. When property is held in tenancy by the entirety, neither spouse can transfer his or her share of the property while alive. The property must go to the surviving spouse. It therefore avoids probate. There are other differences too. Property that is held in tenancy by the entirety is better protected from creditors than is joint tenancy property. If someone sues one spouse and wins the case, property held in tenancy by the entirety cannot be seized to fulfill the judgment. Also, if one spouse has to file for bankruptcy, tenancy by the entirety property is protected from confiscation by creditors.

Nineteen (19) states offer tenancy by the entirety for any asset, and seven additional states offer it for real estate only. Tenancy by the entirety is an attractive option worth asking about the next time you open an account at a financial institution or make a purchase of a car or real estate that requires registration, title, or deed.

The states offering Tenancy by the Entirety are: Arkansas, Connecticut, Delaware, District of Columbia, Hawaii, Maryland, and Massachusetts. Also Vermont, Wyoming, Mississippi, Missouri, New Jersey, Oklahoma, Pennsylvania, Rhode Island, Tennessee, Virginia, and Ohio (if created before 4/04/85). The following states have tenancy by the entirety for real estate only: Alaska, Illinois, Indiana, Kentucky, Michigan, New York, North Carolina, Oregon, and Utah.

THE WRONG JOINT OWNERSHIP RESULTS IN PROBATE

Tenancy In Common

If you live in a state where you must request the right of survivorship in writing when you open a joint account, and you fail to make that request or fail to fill out the proper paperwork, you account will not be a joint tenancy account. The account will be known as a tenancy in common and will not avoid probate when either owner dies.

No matter where you live, any property you own with anyone else, but not owned in joint tenancy or in tenancy by the entirety or community property with the right of survivorship added, is generally considered to be in tenancy in common. Tenancy in common property does not avoid probate when either owner dies. If the deed or ownership registration does not show the type of shared ownership, it's probably owned as tenancy in common.

Assets owned in joint tenancy, or tenancy in the entirety, are owned in equal shares by all members of the tenancy. And upon death the deceased's shares go to the survivors of the tenancy. But in tenancy in common, the shares may be unequal. Any owner can give away his share to anyone else while he lives, and can name any person, charity, or trust in his will to receive his share when he dies. Of course, that property goes to the death beneficiary through probate.

If you and your spouse live in a community property state which does not offer right of survivorship (Idaho, Louisiana, New Mexico, and Washington) the community property you own together (as tenants in common) does not avoid probate when one spouse dies.

If you are not married and you own property with someone else you probably own it as tenants in common. Trying to avoid probate for your share of tenancy in common property by naming a pay-on-death beneficiary to receive it may be impossible. It would be more reliable and less confusing to own the property separately and name a pay-on-death beneficiary to receive it. (Pay-on-death is the subject of the next chapter).

ADVANTAGES OF JOINT OWNERSHIP

Joint ownership is easy to understand and implement. Perhaps that is why it is so commonly accepted. Every strategy has its advantages, and of course there are advantages to joint ownership. They are:

- Easy and Simple. Joint ownership is easy to establish and costs nothing. The paperwork is simple and straightforward.

- Universal. It works for just about everything you own: cars, boats, bank accounts, stocks, bonds, brokerage accounts, real estate, and a lot more.

- Automatic Transfer to the Survivor. Upon the death of a joint owner, the assets held in joint tenancy or any of the other methods with right of survivorship pass directly to the surviving owner(s) automatically by law. The last surviving owner can easily claim the property by presenting his or her identification and a death certificate of the deceased owner.

- More Than Two Joint Tenants Allowed. You can have more than two joint tenants. All will own equal shares.

- Protection From Claims. Joint tenancy property is usually exempt from claims against a deceased member of the tenancy.

- More Protection From Creditors. Tenancy by the entirety property is usually subject only to the creditor claims in which both spouses are responsible for the debt.

DISADVANTAGES OF JOINT OWNERSHIP

There are disadvantages to joint ownership. Fortunately there is a remedy for each.

Creditors

Property held in joint tenancy is subject to the claims of creditors regardless of who is responsible for the debt. If one tenant is a debtor, has claims against him, owes back taxes, or is likely to be sued, joint tenancy puts the assets of all tenants at risk. **The Remedy**: Joint tenancy is not desirable under these circumstances. Consider holding assets separately. To avoid bank account levies by the IRS or capture of assets by creditors, the debtor should consider consulting an attorney about asset protection.

Equal Share Only

Joint tenancy shares and shares under tenancy by the entirety must be equal. **The Remedy**: If you want to own unequal shares (of real estate for example) then see an attorney.

First Yes, Last No

Probate is delayed when the first owner dies. The property merely passes to the surviving owner(s). But the last surviving owner must take action, such as naming a beneficiary for the asset, to avoid probate upon his or her death. This takes time, may be inconvenient, or the need to take action may get overlooked. **The Remedy**: When the joint ownership is created, designate a pay-on-death or transfer-on-death beneficiaries to receive the asset when the last owner dies. A beneficiary designation can be added or changed at any time. Your living trust would be a great choice of beneficiary.

The Unintended Gift

Putting solely owned property in joint tenancy with someone else for the reason of convenience, or to avoid probate, results in a gift of one half interest in the property. When gifts from any person to another person exceed $15,000 in 2018, a gift tax return is supposed to be filed. Example: June's husband died recently, so June created a new deed which put her home in joint tenancy with her son. A gift tax return must be filed with the IRS even though a tax will not be due until the amount of the gift exceeds the federal estate tax exemption threshold. The gift tax return, IRS Form 709 United States Gift (and Generation-Skipping Transfer) Tax Return is an ugly document. Avoid it. (In my opinion all IRS forms are ugly). Also, the new owner could sell or mortgage his or her share, or lose all shares of the joint tenancy to the claims of creditors. This creates a mess. **The Remedy**: Be very selective when you add a new joint tenant. If you add a family member as a joint tenant on your checking account so you can get help managing your everyday finances and paying bills, that's okay, but keep the account balance small. (See the Convenience Checking Account in Chapter 13). Also, instead of adding the name of a new joint owner to the deed for your home, the home should be transferred by deed to your living trust. To avoid probate, hold real estate in your living trust. (See Chapter 7, The Living Trust.)

You Could Lose the Advantage
of Stepped-up Tax Basis

When you make a spouse the joint owner of property you own separately, the surviving spouse could loose an income tax break. For example: Karl purchased stock for $40,000. By the time he married Ann
the stock was worth $60,000. He put the stock in a brokerage account
owned jointly by him and Ann. When Karl died the stock was worth
$100,000, and when Ann sold the stock it was worth $120,000. Ann
will owe tax on the sale price ($120,000 minus the cost basis $40,000).
She will owe tax on $80,000. Instead, if Karl had held the stock sepa-
rately and named Ann as the pay-on-death beneficiary, she would inherit the stock tax free and pay tax on the sale price ($120,000) minus
the stepped-up value of the stock when Karl died, ($100,000). That is a
huge tax savings. **The Remedy:** Hold separate property separately and
name a pay-on-death beneficiary to receive it.

The Lost Federal Estate Tax Exemption

Joint tenancy spouses lose their right to a federal estate tax exemption.
The assets of the first joint tenant to die pass to the survivor. When
the survivor dies, she uses her right to the federal estate tax exemption—one exemption. However, when the married couple creates an
AB Trust, they provide for themselves the future use of two exemptions. When the first spouse dies, the AB Trust will be split into two
trusts. The deceased spouse's property will go into Trust A, the bypass
trust or family trust, with the kids named as eventual beneficiaries. The
survivor's property will go into Trust B, the marital trust. Upon the
death of the second spouse each trust gets to use the federal estate tax
exemption. Trust A gets an exemption, and trust B gets an exemption
too. In 2018 the exemption limit is $11.2 million; a total of $22.4
million for the married couple. Taking advantage of both exemptions
could be a tax savings for some estates. (See estate taxes in Chapter
14). **The Remedy:** Hold assets in your living trust. Plan to make it an
AB Trust if your net estate approaches the federal estate tax exemption
limit. (The AB trust is discussed in Chapter 9).

Breaking a Joint Tenancy

In some states, particularly those with no joint tenancy survivorship clause, the death of a joint tenant may not automatically break (terminate) a joint tenancy, allowing the survivor to safely quitclaim property to his or her living trust, or sell the property. **The Remedy**: If the joint tenancy does not include right of survivorship, ask an attorney if it is necessary to prepare a document to break the joint tenancy.

Losing Your Stuff
Because of Joint Tenancy

The first person to die may lose control over who ultimately receives his or her assets. For example: A surviving spouse owns the property which once belonged to the deceased spouse. If the surviving spouse remarries, what once belonged to the first to die now belongs to a perfect stranger. This is a great way to unintentionally disinherit the children from your first marriage. **The Remedy**: If you own separate property that you want to go to specific persons after your death, hold the property as sole owner and name a beneficiary to receive it. Or hold the property in your living trust, and state in the trust who shall receive it.

Simultaneous Death Is Terrible

Probate is almost guaranteed if the joint owners suffer simultaneous death, which is defined as the condition in which it cannot be determined who died first. Estate planners tell us that simultaneous death is rare and thus not a great concern. Well it isn't, except for the estates of the individuals who suffer it. **The Remedy**: To protect your assets from probate in case of simultaneous death, name a beneficiary to receive your jointly held property.

The "Almost" Simultaneous Death Is Terrible Also

Much more common—in fact frequent—is what I call "almost" simultaneous death. In these cases the joint owners do not die simultaneously but experience somewhat closely spaced deaths. The interval could be a few minutes or several weeks—perhaps several months. Example: John and Beth were driving west in Missouri looking forward to a visit with their grandkids in Kansas. They had a terrible accident. John died instantly and Beth was hospitalized with serious injuries. The family was in turmoil. Sadly, after several weeks Beth passed away. The property John and Beth held as joint tenants or tenants by the entirety became Beth's property automatically, but no one thought of doing additional estate planning before Beth died. There wasn't time or opportunity. As a result Beth's estate had to go through probate resulting in the nightmares and cost that are part of the probate process. There are countless cases in which joint owners' deaths occur in a short time span. Unless they do the proper planning their estates will go through probate. **The Remedy**: The action for probate avoidance in the case of "almost simultaneous death" is the same as for simultaneous death. Always name a beneficiary to receive your jointly held assets.

The Runaway Spouse

Joint tenants can break the tenancy at any time. Your spouse can clean out the checking account—her half and yours—and run away with the plumber. Sorry. Have a nice day. **The Remedy**: Vet the plumber.

Chapter Six

NAME A BENEFICIARY

The Second of the Three Ways To Avoid Probate

WHEN YOU DESIGNATE A beneficiary to receive an asset, you make a contractual arrangement with the financial institution where the asset is held to transfer the asset to the named beneficiary at your death. Naming a beneficiary is a simple process. You may already have gained experience with this procedure at an early age. When you delivered newspapers or had a business mowing lawns in your neighborhood, you probably opened an account at the bank near your home so you could safeguard your extraordinary earnings. You probably listed your mom as the account beneficiary.

Any time you make an investment, start a pension plan, or create paper that represents an asset of value, you should name a beneficiary. You should name a beneficiary to receive the asset whether solely owned or jointly owned. Do it when you acquire the asset. This eliminates the need to make a beneficiary designation later at an inopportune time after a joint owner dies.

When you open a joint account, and the provision to name a beneficiary is not automatically offered, you should inquire if it is permitted. Then insist on making the designation. If you fail to name a beneficiary to receive the asset it will eventually go through probate on its way to your heirs. The process could be a headache for your executor and an additional expense during the settlement of your estate.

Beneficiary designation is a will substitute. Assets for which you designate a beneficiary are removed from your will and automatically avoid probate. The named beneficiary has no right to the asset while you live. You can change the name of the beneficiary or sell the asset whenever you wish. Here are the assets for which you should name a beneficiary:

- Accounts at banks, credit unions, savings and loan associations
- Certificates of Deposit
- Trusts and financial management accounts at banks and trust companies
- Brokerage accounts
- Life insurance policies
- Disability Policies.
- Annuities
- IRAs (Individual retirement accounts)
- Pension plans of all types. These include 401(k), 403b Defined Benefit Pension Plans; Profit Sharing Plans, Defined Contributions, Keogh Plans.
- Tax favored savings plans
- Health savings accounts
- Private placement agreements
- Venture funding agreements
- Real Estate (in 9 states only)
- Vehicles (in 5 states currently)

Most of the assets above can be designated to pay-on-death (P.O.D.) to a designated beneficiary, or several beneficiaries. These P.O.D. assets avoid probate and go to the designated beneficiary.

The beneficiary designation of the brokerage account is slightly different. Rather than P.O.D., the brokerage account in most states may be designated to transfer-on-death (T.O.D.) to a named beneficiary. The T.O.D. beneficiaries, whether persons or trusts, inherit the account and assume management of the assets. The beneficiaries can trade the account or sell the assets whenever they choose.

In five states vehicles can be titled to transfer-on-death to a designated beneficiary. That is an option to consider if it is available in your state. (Read about these vehicle transfers in chapter 16).

In nine states you can name a beneficiary to receive real estate by using a Revocable Transfer-on-Death Deed. It is an option that may serve your needs. I personally prefer to hold real estate in a living trust. (The details are in chapter 16).

Whom Do You Name as a Beneficiary?

Beneficiaries can be persons, corporations, charities, your college, all kinds of trusts, including your living trust. The list is endless. It is essential that you name the beneficiary so the asset will avoid probate.

Most people make a list of potential beneficiaries. They start with their spouse and children. The next level would probably be siblings and parents, and then nieces and nephews. It doesn't matter whom you choose so long as you don't attempt to exclude a spouse or child who has a legal right to their share of the property. If you wish to exclude someone whom you suspect may have legal right, consult an attorney.

Yes, you can name children as beneficiaries. You need to name a guardian to care for your minor children after you die. That is accomplished when you make your will. You also need to name a custodian to manage the children's property. The selection of the financial custodian is also made in your will.

If you name beneficiaries for all your assets, or you hold the assets in your living trust, your estate will be a non-probate estate. If your children are still minors upon your death, your executor can advise the court that your will is not being filed for probate, and court involvement is only for the purpose of approving the guardian and custodian selections you made. If you made a pour-over will—and most attorneys suggest a pour-over will in addition to your living trust—your beneficiaries named in the trust will receive the assets. The names of the beneficiaries and the assets they receive will remain private.

P.O.D. AND T.O.D. DESIGNATIONS

Opening a pay-on-death account at your bank or other financial institutions is very simple and in most cases costs nothing. Provide your name and address and social security number so the IRS can tax any interest. Be sure to designate a beneficiary or more than one if you wish. This is a great way to keep money—even large amounts of it—out of probate. As long as you are alive the named beneficiary has no right to the money. You can spend the money, change the name of the beneficiary, or close the account.

Pay-on-Death (P.O.D.) designations are frequently used on bank accounts, stocks and bonds, and most of the assets listed above. However, brokerage accounts are usually designated transfer-on-death (T.O.D.) to designated beneficiaries.

If John Wilson wants to leave a bank account to his children he can use this language:

"John Wilson P.O.D. to John Wilson Jr. and Sarah H. Wilson."

In this case John leaves the account in equal shares to John Jr. and Sarah. If Sarah marries and changes her name she still collects her share when John dies; she was a Wilson when the designation was made. If one of the children predeceases John all of the account will go to the child who survives, free of probate. If both children predecease John, and John fails to designate a new beneficiary, the account becomes a probate asset. That's not a happy outcome. However, if John had designated his living trust as beneficiary the outcome would be much better. Living trusts don't die; the account remains a non-probate asset.

Some states do not permit leaving unequal shares to multiple designees. And in most cases you can't name alternate beneficiaries. John should consider naming his living trust as beneficiary if he wants to leave unequal shares or name alternate beneficiaries. In his trust he can state the unequal shares amounts he wants the final beneficiaries and alternate beneficiaries to receive. He can name the trust as beneficiary in this manner:

"John Wilson P.O.D. to the trustee(s) of the John Wilson Living Trust dated 7-15-2008."

John is not giving the asset to the trustees as individuals, but to his trust, where the successor trustees (very likely he named John Jr. and Sarah as co-successor trustees) will serve as trustees after John's death. The living trust directs who gets what. John Jr. and Sarah will distribute the trust assets to themselves and others in accordance with the designations in the trust.

If John Wilson wants to probate-proof his brokerage account, he can leave it T.O.D. to his children or to his living trust:

"John Wilson T.O.D. to John Wilson Jr. and Sarah Wilson."

Since many brokerage firms impose a significant fee if you list more than one T.O.D. beneficiary, it would be wise to ask about their fee schedule. In any event, a better and completely private transfer will be possible if you name your living trust as the beneficiary:

"John Wilson T.O.D. to the trustee(s) of the John Wilson Living Trust dated 7-15-2008."

Of course John can designate other trusts to receive assets. For example:

"John Wilson P.O.D. to the trustee for the Legacy Trust of Ralph E. Smith dated 4-13-2004." And anyone can easily leave an account or asset to charity: *"John Wilson P.O.D. to the American Cancer Society."*

WARNING: Don't make it too difficult for the holder of the asset. The following designation could be too much for a bank or brokerage:

"John Wilson P.O.D. to my friend Patrick Smyth of Noplace, Nebraska, one third, and Andrew Roberts, of Noplace, Nebraska, two thirds. Should one predecease me, all to the other. Should both predecease me 100 percent shall go to the Water Street Rescue Mission in Smithers, Kansas."

The bequeath above should go in your trust. Make the asset P.O.D. to your trust and the trustee can make the distributions to Nebraska or Kansas (if necessary).

If for some reason you are not permitted to hold an asset in the manner you wish or name the beneficiary of your choice, consider holding the asset in your trust. As an example, you may not name a P.O.D. beneficiary to receive a government bond if you hold the bond in joint names. (See government bonds in chapter 16).

P.O.D. and T.O.D. beneficiaries can easily claim assets. Simply present personal identification and a copy of the death certificate to the custodian of the asset where the account is held. Payment or transfer should be prompt. If any financial institution asks for a copy of your trust, give it a copy of the Certificate of Trust (also known as an Abstract of Trust). A certificate of trust is a legal document which certifies that a specific trust exists. It is created at the same time you create your living trust.

Name a Beneficiary For Your Jointly Held Accounts

Many married couples, and unmarried as well, hold assets in joint names. And that's it. They believe that's all that is necessary, because joint ownership is a way to avoid probate. That is true unless both die at the same time or closely together, or one owner dies and the survivor fails to take action to name a beneficiary for the asset. To avoid probate, always designate a beneficiary to receive your jointly held assets. The beneficiary will not receive the asset until after the last joint owner dies.

Consider naming your living trust as beneficiary. Name your living trust to receive bank accounts, brokerage accounts, and just about any asset you own.

To convince you that jointly held bank accounts are seldom designated pay-on-death to a living trust, here is a true story. Twenty-five years ago my wife and I lived in the upscale town of Jackson, Wyoming. Yes, Virginia, there are upscale places west of the Hudson River. Yes, even west of Laramie.

The checking account in Wyoming received periodic deposits, and the bank paid higher than average interest on the account balance, so we decided to keep the account open after we moved to South Dakota. I wrote a letter to the bank asking that our living trust be designated a P.O.D. beneficiary, and I enclosed a copy of the Certificate of Trust.

To show you how unusual yet sensible this request was, here is the verbatim answer from the bank: *"Dear Mr. Sam -------, Thank you for sending a copy of your trust papers to us. We have consulted a few people on the matter of adding your trust as the beneficiary to your account. We have found that in the state of Wyoming our laws do not include a trust as a beneficiary but they also do not exclude a trust. Therefore, we will go ahead and add your trust to your account as the beneficiary."*

This bank is a large, profitable and growing state chartered bank. They should have known that a trust can—and should—be designated as a beneficiary for any account. This event suggests a trust is seldom designated as a beneficiary for jointly held accounts. Sure, the Wyoming laws don't exclude a trust as a beneficiary. Trusts aren't excluded anywhere; they are accepted as a beneficiary in every state. Yes, you can use your living trust as a beneficiary for a whole host of assets, whether you own the asset solely or jointly. It is a sensible solution. Plan on it, and do it.

Whether you hold the asset in your living trust now, or have it pay-on-death to your living trust after your death, the result is the same. It becomes a trust asset now or later. No probate.

ADVANTAGES OF P.O.D. AND T.O.D. DESIGNATIONS

The **Advantages** of beneficiary designation are:

- **Easy and Simple.** It is easy to do. It takes very little extra time to name a beneficiary when you open an account. Place the name of the beneficiary on the registration document. All custodians have forms available for this purpose. Upon your death the beneficiary identifies himself or herself to the custodian of the asset and provides a copy of the death certificate. The asset will be promptly paid or transferred to the beneficiary.

- **The Asset Avoids Probate.** The asset avoids probate so long as a beneficiary remains alive. (See "A Beneficiary Dies" below).

THE DISADVANTAGES OF P.O.D. AND T.O.D. DESIGNATIONS

The **Disadvantages** of beneficiary designation are:

- **A Beneficiary Dies.** If the beneficiary dies, you need to name a new beneficiary or move the asset into your trust. If you fail to make this change, the asset will ultimately go through probate.

- **Record Keeping**. You need to keep an up to date record of your designated beneficiaries. This could be complicated if you named a large number of beneficiaries to receive your possessions.

- **Change of Mind.** If you change your mind about a beneficiary, you will need to contact the custodians holding the asset and make the change or numerous changes. This involves time and paperwork.

- **Loss of Privacy.** The custodians holding your assets learn the names of your beneficiaries and who gets what. Forget about privacy. By contrast, the names of the beneficiaries listed in your trust remain private.

- **Distribution Confusion.** Your will and living trust state specific amounts or shares your beneficiaries shall receive. Sometimes these amounts may differ. In addition, when you bequeath specific assets to pay-on-death beneficiaries you may easily violate the shares specifications. (See Distribution Confusion on page 117). **Remedy:** Naming your living trust as the designated beneficiary for you assets, or simply holding the assets in your living trust, eliminates the disadvantages above. (Recommendations on what to hold in your trust are made in chapter 16).

AVOID BENEFICIARY MISTAKES

Retirement plans, including IRAs, 401(k)s, 403(b)s, and the federal government's Thrift Savings Plan all allow you to name a beneficiary to receive your assets when you die. Avoid these common and costly errors:

- **Naming your estate as your beneficiary**. Don't name your estate as a beneficiary. Name individuals instead. The tax code provides named beneficiaries with more tax-friendly choices than when they receive your IRA through your trust or through the probate process. So plan to name individuals. Ask your attorney for guidance on this matter.

- **Failure to keep your designations current.** Review and update your beneficiaries each time you experience a major life event such as marriage, the birth or adoption of a child, divorce, retirement, or the death of a beneficiary.

- **Minors can't own investments outright**. Minors need an adult to serve as custodian until they reach the age of majority. The custodian is named in your will. Make sure that gets done.

AN ADDITIONAL THOUGHT

Naming your living trust as a designated beneficiary gets little emphasis from lawyers who write books about wills, trusts, and estate planning. In my opinion your living trust is in most cases the best beneficiary you can name to receive the assets. The exception is retirement accounts. For retirement accounts you should name a person as beneficiary. Naming your trust to receive all your other assets eliminates a serious problem which I call Distribution Confusion (see page 117).

Failure to name a beneficiary can allow an asset to "pay into your estate." Attorneys who tell you that an asset will "pay into your estate" are talking about a probate estate. A probate estate is unacceptable. Name beneficiaries.

CHAPTER SEVEN

THE LIVING TRUST

The Third of the Three Ways
To Avoid Probate

MOST OF US KNOW very little about the living trust. We think that the trust is a complex legal device used only by the wealthy and available only from a specially trained trust attorney. Not true. It is neither complex nor difficult. Any one can create a living trust privately and inexpensively.

WHAT IS A LIVING TRUST?

A Living Trust is a legal entity, which can hold property in the same manner as other legal entities such as partnerships and corporations. A person (the **"grantor"**) creates a trust and transfers his property to the trust. A **"trustee"** administers the trust for the benefit of the **"beneficiary."** The grantor, trustee, and beneficiary may be, and usually are, the same person.

Here is an example: Charles Clarke, the grantor, creates a living trust. He transfers his property to the designated trustee of the trust, Charles Clarke, who manages the trust property. Charles, as trustee, adds property to the trust and sells trust property whenever he choses. He does this for the benefit of the beneficiary, Charles Clarke. When Charles dies the person designated in the trust as successor trustee distributes the trust property to the final beneficiaries of the trust. It sounds like a scam, but it's proper, legal, and effective. Who would have devised such a scheme? Only lawyers. Let's give the lawyers credit. Thank you. And kudos.

The **Grantor** is also called the **Trustor**, and sometimes the **Settlor.** The terms are interchangeable. In this book we use the term "grantor".

Married couples, as grantors, can create a shared living trust, also known as a joint living trust, or marital trust. In this book we use the term joint living trust. The grantors serve as co-trustees

The trust avoids probate by having title of the property in the name of the trustee(s) and not in the name of the decedent(s) at the time of death. Upon the death of the grantor(s), the trust becomes **irrevocable** and the new trustee, who was named as successor trustee in the trust document, has the authority to pay the decedent's bills and has a fiduciary responsibility to distribute the trust property to final beneficiaries.

When the grantor(s) create their living trust they specify the powers of the trustee(s). These powers allow the trustee(s) to fully manage all the trust property. The grantor(s) also name a successor trustee or successor co-trustees to serve after the grantors' deaths, and alternate successor trustees to serve if the first choice is unavailable or unwilling to serve. Thus there is always someone available to manage the trust property and settle the trust after a grantor's death.

The trust usually permits the successor trustee to act on behalf of the grantor should the grantor become incapacitated during his lifetime. This guarantees that a competent person remains in control. A Durable Power-of-Attorney document is recommended to give similar power, if necessary, to a trusted person to manage assets not transferred to the trust.

The living trust is not a complicated document. It is no more complicated than a will. But there is a huge benefit in having a living trust. Upon the death of the grantor(s), property held in the trust goes to the death beneficiaries without probate.

The revocable living trust is the only devise that can be used with all types of property and does not depend on survival of specific persons. Because the living trust is a private document that grants the trustees complete control of the trust property, the trustee's duties are carried out privately without lawyers, courts, court fees, or judges.

The living trust is incredibly useful. There are many reasons for having one. Here is an example: A decade ago Susie Graham made a new will. She named her daughter, Nancy, as executor. After Susie died, Nancy decided to sell her mother's house. Nancy listed the house with a realtor who promptly found a buyer.

When real estate is sold, the seller (the person holding the deed) must provide and sign a new deed in favor of the buyer. But Susie is deceased and could not sign the deed. Therefore, someone else must sign. That person, in Susie's case, was the person designated as executor of Susie's will, Nancy. But Nancy can't sign until she gets an appointment from the probate court. To get this appointment, Nancy had to file her mother's will for probate, get Letters Testamentary from the court, and a court appointment as executor. Only then could Nancy prepare and sign a new deed. This was probate with the inconveniences that go with it.

If Susie had created a living trust and put her home in her name as trustee of her living trust, then Nancy, as the successor trustee, could prepare and sign the new deed. No courts, judges, or lawyers. Perfect.

ADVANTAGES OF THE LIVING TRUST

There are a lot of advantages to the living trust, and few perceived disadvantages. The advantages first:

Avoids Probate. The living trust is available to everyone, whether single, married, or unmarried couples. Property held in the living trust avoids probate. The property goes directly to the heirs and beneficiaries. The cost of probate and delay in settling the estate under probate—on average a year or more—are the primary reasons for having a living trust. The trust is settled privately and there is no oversight by any government, court, or judge. For example, when multimillionaire Bing Crosby died in 1978 with his assets in a living trust, the public never learned much about his vast estate or who received the assets. The trust was settled privately.

Simplicity. Many people think the living trust is too complicated and difficult to understand. That is not true. Anyone with a sixth grade education can understand the living trust. (Well, maybe eighth grade). The living trust is easy to create, and managing the trust assets is not difficult. Although the living trust is a separate entity from the grantor, so long as the grantor is alive and serving as trustee, all income generated by the trust is reported as income on the grantor's IRS Form 1040 Individual Income Tax Return.

Privacy. The living trust remains private. If a county Register of Deeds or your bank asks for a copy—when your trust leases a safe deposit box, for example—give them an Abstract of Trust or a Certification of Trust which certifies that a valid living trust exists. Alternately, you can give them the pages of the trust that lists the names of the grantor(s), the trustee(s), and the powers of the trustees. You never have to reveal the specifics of the trust property or the final beneficiaries.

Stability. Living trusts normally do not need to be altered if you move to another state.

Continual Management. A major benefit of the living trust is its assurance of competent management. If the trustee becomes incompetent, the designated successor trustee can take over and manage the trust property without delay or court assistance. In the case of the joint living trust, if a co-trustee becomes disabled, the trust allows the remaining co-trustee to serve alone. For example: Ron and Laura held title to their home as joint tenants. When Ron developed Alzheimer's disease, he needed more care than Laura could provide him by herself. Ron had to be moved to a special dementia facility, and Laura had to put their home up for sale in order to pay for his care. When a buyer was found, Ron was unable to sign the new deed. So Laura had to arrange for a court-appointed conservator to represent Ron at the closing. If Ron and Laura had held their home in a joint living trust, the provisions of the trust could allow Laura to serve alone as trustee and sign the new deed. Court involvement would not have been necessary. If both Ron and Laura became disabled, the successor trustee would serve. Again, there would be no court involvement in trust management.

The AB Trust Can Reduce Taxes. Living trusts do not save on income taxes. Neither does a will. You still have to pay tax on income. But the AB trust created by a married couple can save federal estate taxes levied on large estates and state inheritance taxes too. After the first spouse dies, the trust assets are split into two trusts, trusts A and B, with the surviving spouse owning only the B trust. Upon the death of the second spouse both trusts pass to the final beneficiaries, usually the children. Each trust receives the federal estate tax exemption resulting in the possible saving of thousand of dollars. (Read about the AB Trust in more detail in Chapter 9).

Available to All Couples. All couples can use the living trust. Unfortunately, unmarried couples are not entitled to the "marital deduction" which provides that all property left or given to a surviving spouse is exempt from estate or gift tax. Any amount either unmarried partner owns in excess of the personal estate tax exemption will be subject to tax when that person dies. However, unmarried couples can achieve overall tax savings with a bypass trust, but in this case the trust isn't called an AB trust. Rather, it is simply called a bypass trust or life estate trust. And significant tax savings are available to you. You can read all about bypass trusts in estate planning manuals, but questions will remain. An estate planning attorney can answer these questions and suggest tax savings.

Discourages Litigation. Living trusts discourage litigation. Although lawsuits are possible, there are no court proceedings to support a contest by creditors or dissatisfied beneficiaries. Distribution of the trust assets to the beneficiaries is non-judicial, so proceeding with a lawsuit is difficult. If Charles Kuralt, the late CBS-TV personally, had held his estate in in a living trust, the notorious and expensive lawsuit between his wife and mistress over his ranch in Montana would probably never have occurred.

DISADVANTAGES OF THE LIVING TRUST

There are no certifiable disadvantages to the living trust. Nonetheless, here are the **perceived** disadvantages.

Cost. The primary argument against creating a living trust is the perceived high cost. The accepted belief is you pay now (when you create the trust) or your estate pays later (when the estate goes through probate), and the cost is about the same. Many claim it is cheaper and easier to write a will instead. These ideas are FALSE. You can create your living trust for pennies on the dollar compared to the cost and inconvenience of probate. And if you need a will (and attorneys claim everyone should have one), you can write your will at the same time for no extra cost. Neither is expensive. So cost is not an excuse for not having a trust. (How to create your trust and its cost are discussed at length in Chapter 10).

The Inexperienced Trustee. Some attorneys suggest that a probate judge become involve in overseeing the operation of the living trust and thereby ensure the trustee's interests and the interests of his loved ones. What they really mean is that an attorney should oversee what the trustee does. This is a good idea if the grantor (who is also is serving as the trustee) is fiscally inept. But it is unlikely someone that inept would have been smart enough to create the trust in the first place. These attorneys are expressing self-interest and seeking fees. Of course the trustee should always consult an attorney when management questions arise, but otherwise an attorney need not be involved.

Paperwork. Another complaint is there is too much paperwork required in funding and managing the trust. This concern is overblown. Yes, the trustee needs to transfer some property from himself as owner to himself as trustee of the trust. This is a one-time event for just the few assets you decide to move to the trust. The transfer is not difficult. Other assets can be titled to the trust when they are acquired. Very seldom is additional paperwork required after the assets have been placed in trust.

Refinance. Another complaint about the living trust is the fact that when refinancing real estate some mortgage lenders require the title be taken out of the living trust so the borrower, rather than the borrower as trustee, can sign the paperwork. This is a ridiculous requirement. Nonetheless, it is not a big issue, and the transfer of title is simple. Banks, mortgage brokers, title companies, and lawyers understand this and do it all the time for customers. The cost is small. After the refinancing is completed, the title is put back in the trust. Again, this practice is ridiculous and annoying. But now that you know about this requirement, you can be prepared to accept this aggravation when it happens. As another approach, you might offer to show the lender a copy of your trust document which specifically gives you as trustee the power to borrow against trust property. If you can't convince the lender to deal with you as the trustee, you can threaten to find another lender, or just suck it up and agree to their ridiculous double transfer demand.

Medicaid Eligibility. Creating a trust can significantly affect your eligibility for Medicaid to pay for nursing home care. If you create a trust naming yourself or your spouse as beneficiaries, and you do it within five years of the time you need to apply for Medicaid, you may be ineligible for the benefit. Assets in trust are considered available for you to spend on your nursing home costs even if you receive no payments from the trust. The remedy: create your living trust now. Don't delay.

DO I NEED A LIVING TRUST?

You might rephrase the question, "What would I use a living trust for?" Good question. If you can answer "yes" to any of the following examples, you need one.

If you own real estate you need a living trust. Here's why. When real estate is sold the seller must prepare and sign a deed in favor of the buyer. Obviously, if the seller is deceased he cannot sign. The real estate must then go through probate. The probate court will appoint an executor who will serve on behalf of the seller and sign the new deed. Conversely, if the property was held in a trust the successor trustee will sign the new deed. No probate, no probate fee, no probate court.

Yes, it is true that in a few states (nine at this writing) you can name a beneficiary to receive real estate upon your death. Even if that option is available to you it may not be a good choice. You could be giving a large share of your estate to one person, one of your children for example, at the expense of the other children. That may not be what you really intended. (See Distribution Confusion discussed in chapter 15). When you hold real estate in trust, the proceeds from the sale of the real estate will be distributed after your death to beneficiaries in accordance with instructions in your trust. No probate court is involved.

Frankly, it is worth creating a trust simply to use it as a P.O.D. beneficiary. Name your living trust as a P.O.D. (or T.O.D.) beneficiary to receive assets—all types of assets—after your death. In my opinion this is one of the most important uses of your trust. The trust does not own the asset, but is simply designated as the pay-on-death beneficiary. If this is all you intend to use the trust for that is quite acceptable. Whether your trust owns the asset, or you merely name the trust as P.O.D. beneficiary to receive the asset upon your death, the outcome is the same. The asset avoids probate. And don't forget to name your trust as P.O.D. beneficiary for all your jointly held assets too, with the exception of real estate of course, which should be held be in your trust.

If you want to name your trust as a P.O.D. beneficiary, but rules for an asset do not permit this, then hold the asset in your trust instead. Government bonds are an example. The United States Government does not permit naming a trust as P.O.D. beneficiary for their bonds. So hold the bonds in your trust.

Do you have a safe deposit box? If your trust leases the box and the trustee pays the rent, then the trustee (you) can enter the box while you live, and your successor trustee can enter unobstructed after your death. If you fail to use your trust as lessee, your executor may need to contact the probate court for "help" getting entry into the box. Typically your executor will wait at the bank until a state bureaucrat arrives and grants permission, and then watches intently to find something the state can tax. The practice is a disgusting and disgraceful invasion of privacy.

DOES THE SIZE OF YOUR ESTATE
DICTATE THE NEED FOR A LIVING TRUST?

I recently responded to an offer to be shown a new way to avoid probate. I thought I would learn something. A salesman arrived at our house and quickly admitted he was selling life insurance annuities. Life insurance, whether term, whole life, or annuities are contractual arrangements whereby the beneficiary receives the death benefit upon the death of the insured, free of probate. I asked him if a trust wouldn't be a better way to avoid probate. He asked, "How large is the estate?" I threw out the number $650,000. His response, "That estate is too small to need a trust."

He obviously knew very little about estate planning and probate avoidance. The primary reason for having a living trust is to avoid the cost and aggravation of probate. The size of one's estate has absolutely nothing to do with the need for a living trust. A small estate needs a living trust too. A small estate can least afford the cost of probate.

Chapter Eight

THE DECLARATION OF TRUST

THE DOCUMENT THAT CREATES THE TRUST

The revocable living trust commonly used to avoid probate is known as the inter-vivos trust. The Latin literally means **between** (inter) and **living persons** (vivos).

The living trust is easy to create. Whether you create the living trust at you attorney's office, do it online at a website like LegalZoom, or do it in the privacy of you home, the document will be created using computer software. The texts may vary slightly, but all will define the terms of the trust. They will name the grantors, trustees, successor trustees and the beneficiaries. And they will enumerate the powers granted the trustees. The powers will allow the trustees to fully manage the trust assets.

TYPES OF LIVING TRUSTS

The first is the Basic Living Trust. It is used by the individual who creates a trust as sole grantor, or by couples who, as joint grantors, create a joint living trust, also known as the shared living trust. In this book we use the term joint living trust. (CONTINUED ON NEXT PAGE)

The second type of living trust is the estate tax-reducing AB Trust. This trust benefits the small percentage of married couples whose estate value exceeds the federal estate tax threshold. These trusts can reduce or eliminate federal estate tax and possibly reduce state death tax as well. (The AB Trust is discussed in chapter 9).

The Basic Living Trust For The Individual

The basic living trust is commonly used by unmarried persons of all ages, such as single parents and widows and widowers, and sometimes by married persons who have separate property they wish to keep separate. The trusts they create all avoid probate for the property they transfer to the trusts. The trust document is simple, straightforward, and easy to understand. Here is an example:

Rose was a widow in her 80s. She lived in a beautiful rural community in Iowa. She and her husband had no children. Her favorite heirs were two nieces and a nephew. They were close to her and provided advice and support. In the spring of 1999 Rose made a new will (called a last will and testament). She named her nieces and her nephew, Todd, as beneficiaries of her estate. They were to inherit her estate in equal shares. She named Todd as executor, and her niece, Sally, as alternate executor.

Several months later Rose told Todd she heard horror stories about probate. She wanted none of that. She wanted to avoid probate. Todd agreed.

Todd explained to Rose the problems with probate and how a basic living trust was easy to create and how it would avoid the cost and annoyance of probate. Rose was happy to accept Todd's help.

Todd used living trust software to create the living trust. The beneficiaries were the same as those listed in Rose's will. Since Todd was listed as executor in the will, he was named successor trustee in the trust. The alternate successor trustee was Sally, the same alternate executor listed in the will. This is important: naming the same people in both documents eliminates conflicts. Rose signed the living trust in front of a notary. No witnesses were required.

Rose owned her home and an agency account in the trust department at the local bank, and her car. Todd prepared a quitclaim deed transferring the home from Rose, as sole owner of the real estate, to Rose as trustee of her trust. He recorded the deed at the Register Deeds office at the county courthouse. There was a small recording fee.

Todd wrote a short letter to the bank requesting the agency account be designated P.O.D. to Rose's trust. Rose signed the letter and delivered it to the bank on her next visit. She also provided the bank with a copy of the Certificate of Trust. (Please note that the account was not transferred to the trust, but P.O.D. to the trust). When Rose dies the account will be paid into the trust. With respect to the car, Rose went to her local DMV office and transferred the car to her trust. There was a small fee for this service. Her checking account and other intangible personal property was designated P.O.D. to the trust. The job was finished. Rose had created a non-probate estate. It was easy.

Rose called her trust the Rose Evans Living Trust. She could have called it the Rose Evans Revocable Living Trust, or any name she desired. Some simply call their trust a "Declaration of Trust." The name is the grantor's choice. What is important is the date she signed the document in front of the notary. The name and date identifies the trust.

Rose died in 2006. Todd sold the real estate and the car. He easily settled the trust in less than 30 days.

Note: This is a true story. The names and places were changed. The author of this book was Todd. I was the executor and successor trustee. I settled the trust and promptly distributed the assets to each of the eight beneficiaries. No lawyers or courts were involved.

The Basic Living Trust For Individuals As Partners

Bill and Sally are unmarried partners. Each owns a house, their cars, and their individual bank accounts. Bill converted his house into a rental. They lived in Sally's house. Friends told them about the advantages of living trusts, so Bill bought trust and will writing software and they each created an individual living trust for themselves. Bill was Sally's successor trustee and final beneficiary. Sally was Bill's successor trustee and final beneficiary. They named alternate successor trustees to insure a trustee was available in the event they suffered simultaneous deaths.

Sally transferred her home and car to her trust, and Bill did the same with his rental property and car. Their bank accounts and other assets with registration documents were changed to P.O.D. to their individual trusts. They chose a good system to protect their real estate and personal property from probate. Well done.

The Joint Living Trust

John and Doris Svendson of Harding County, South Dakota, created a joint living trust (also called a shared living trust). John and Doris were dirt poor when they got married during the Middle Ages. They have been together forever, and everything they own they own together. Their trust is very simple, although it appears complex because lawyers wrote it to cover every contingency. Simply, when the last survivor dies everything goes to their kids, John Jr., Jane, and Emily. If the children had been minors the trust would have been slightly more complicated, but not much. In that case they would have created a child's subtrust within their trust. The property inherited by the minor children would be transferred to the custodian the grantors choose. The custodian would manage the property until the child reaches the age specified in the state law, or until the child reaches the age the grantors specify.

The Svendson living trust was created in 2002. It is a living trust in effect today. The grantors are alive and well. It is an example of a typical revocable living trust for a married couple. Readers are invited to change the names and use this trust for themselves.

The John and Doris Svendson Joint Living Trust

This Joint Living Trust Agreement (this "Agreement") between John and Doris Svendson (the "Grantors" or "Beneficiaries") and John and Doris Svendson (collectively, the "Trustee").

In consideration of mutual covenants and promises set forth in this Agreement, the Grantors and the Trustee agree as follows:

I. PURPOSE. The purpose of this Agreement is to establish a Trust to receive and manage assets for the benefit of the Grantors during the Grantors' lifetime, and to further manage and distribute the assets of the Trust upon he death of the surviving Grantor.

II. FUNDING OF TRUST. This trust shall be funded with assets transferred to this trust by either of both of the grantors at the time of creating this trust, or at any later time. Any community property transferred into or out of this Trust shall remain community property until the death of either Grantor and such property, including undistributed income that it generates, shall not be commingled. This Trust may also receive property from any person or entity who is acting under the authority granted to that person or entity by the Grantors. It is expected that this Trust may receive assets pursuant to the terms of either Grantor's Last Will and Testament.

III. MANAGEMENT OF TRUST ASSETS. The trustee shall manage and distribute the trust assets for the benefit of the grantors and their successor(s) in interest in accordance with the terms of this Agreement.

IV. PAYMENTS DURING THE LIFETIMES OF THE GRANTORS. During the joint or survivor lifetimes of the Grantors, the Trustee shall pay all of the net income of this Trust, and also such sums from principal as either Grantor may request

(CONTINUED ON NEXT PAGE)

(CONTINUED)

at any time in writing, to or for the benefit o the Grantors, or as either Grantor may designate. Such payments shall be made at least quarterly. The grantors may change the amounts of the payments at any time by providing written notice to the Trustee. Any excess income shall be added to the principal at the discretion of the Trustee.

   A. *Payments During a "Disability of a Grantor."* During any period that a Grantor has a "disability", the trustee may pay to or for the benefit of such Grantor such amounts of income and principal as the Trustee believes in the Trustee's sole discretion to be required for (i) such Grantor's support and welfare, (ii) such Grantor's accustomed manner of living, or (iii) any purpose that the Trustee believes to be in the best interest of the Grantor.

   B. *Disability Defined.* For the purpose of this Trust, "disability" shall mean a legal disability or the inability to provide prompt and intelligent consideration to financial matters by reason of illness or mental or physical disability. The determination of whether a Grantor has a disability shall be made by such Grantor's most recent attending physician. The Trustee shall be entitled to rely on written notice of that determination.

V. DEATH OF A GRANTOR. Upon the death of the first Grantor to die (the "decedent"). the trust shall become irrevocable with respect to the property contributed to the Trust by the Decedent (including accumulated income on that property, but excluding trust property given to the surviving Grantor) and shall continue for the benefit of the surviving Grantor (the "Surviving Grant-

(CONTINUED ON NEXT PAGE)

or"), subject to distributions (if any) that may be required (i) by this Agreement, or (ii) to pay the just debts, funeral expenses, and expenses of last illness of the Decedent.

A. *Thirty-Day Survival Requirement.* For the purpose of determining the appropriate distributions under this Trust, no person shall be determined to have survived the Grantor making the distribution unless such person is also living on the thirtieth day after the date of that Grantor's death.

B. *Common Disaster.* If the Grantors die under circumstances such that there is no clear or convincing evidence as to the order of their deaths, or it is difficult or impractical to determine which person survived the death of the other person, it shall, for the purpose of distribution of life insurance, property passing under any will or other contracts, if any, and property passing under this Trust, be conclusively presumed that John Svendon predeceased Doris Svendson.

VI. DISTRIBUTION OF RESIDUARY TRUST ASSETS UPON THE SURVIVING GRANTOR'S DEATH. Upon the death of the second Grantor to die (the "Surviving Grantor"), the residuary assets of this Trust shall be distributed to the grantors' children in equal shares. If a child does not survive the Surviving Grantor, such deceased child's share shall be distributed in equal shares to he children of the deceased child who survived by right of representation. If a child does not survive the Surviving Grantor and has no children who so survive, such deceased child's share shall be distributed in equal shares to the grantor's other children, if any, or to their respective children by right of representation.

(CONTINUED ON NEXT PAGE)

(CONTINUED)

If no child of the Grantors' survives the surviving Grantor, and if none of the Grantors' deceased children are survived by children, the residuary assets of this Trust shall be distributed 50.00 % to the heirs-at-law of Doris Svendson and 50.00 % to the heir-in-law of John Svendson.

VII. TRUSTEE POWERS. The Trustee, in addition to other powers and authority granted by law or necessary or appropriate for proper administration of the Trust, shall have the following rights, powers, and authority without order of court and without notice to anyone:

A. *Receive Assets.* To receive, hold, maintain, administer, collect, invest, and reinvest the trust assets, and collect and apply the income, profits, and principal of the Trust in accordance with the terms of the instrument.

B. *Receive Additional Asset.* To receive additional assets from other sources, including assets received under the Will of a Grantor or any other person.

C. *Standard of Care.* To acquire, invest, reinvest, exchange, retain, sell, and manage estate and trust assets, exercising the judgment and care, under the circumstances then prevailing, that persons of prudence, discretion and intelligence exercise in the management of their own affairs, not in regard to speculation but in regard to permanent disposition on their funds, considering the probable income as well as the probable safety of their capital. Within the limitations of that standard, the Trustee is authorized to acquire and retain every kind of property, real, personal or mixed, and every kind of investment,

(CONTINUED ON NEXT PAGE)

specifically including, but not by way of limitation, bonds, debentures and other corporate obligations, and stocks, preferred or common, that persons of prudence, discretion, and intelligence acquire or retain of their own account, even though not a legal investment for trust funds under the laws and statues of the United States or the state under which this instrument in administered.

D. *Retain Assets.* To retain any asset, including uninvited cash or original investments, regardless of whether it is of the kind authorized by this instrument for investment and whether it leaves a disproportionately large part of the estate or trust invested in one type of property, for as long as the Trustee deems advisable.

E. *Dispose of Encumber Assets.* To sell, option, mortgage, pledge, lese, or convey real or personal property, publicly or privately, upon such terms and conditions as may appear to be proper, and to execute all instruments necessary to effect such authority.

F. *Settle Claims.* To compromise, settle, or abandon claims in favor of or against the trust.

G. *Manage Property.* To manage real estate and personal property, borrow money, exercise options, buy insurance, and register insurance as may appear to be proper.

H. *Allocate Between Principal and Income.* To make allocations of charges and credits as between principal and income as in the sole discretion of the Trustee may appear to be proper.

(CONTINUED ON NEXT PAGE)

(CONTINUED)

I. *Employ Professional Assistance.* To employ and compensate counsel and other persons deemed necessary for the proper administration and to delegate authority when such delegation is advantageous to the Trust.

J. *Distribute Property.* To make division or distribution in money or kind, or partly in either, including disproportionate in-kind distributions, at value to be determined by the Trustee. And the Trustee's judgment shall be binding upon all interested parties.

K. *Enter Contracts.* To bind the Trust by contracts or agreements without assuming individual liability for such contracts.

L. *Exercise Stock Ownership Rights.* To vote, execute proxies to vote, join in or oppose any plans for organization, and exercise any other rights incident to the ownership of any stocks, bonds, or other properties of the Trust.

M. *Duration of Powers.* To continue to exercise the powers provided in this agreement after the termination of the Trust until all the assets of the Trust have been distributed.

N. *Hold Trust Assets as a Single Fund.* To hold the assets of the Trust, shares, or portions of the Trust created by this instrument as a single fund for the joint investment and management, without the need for physical segregation, dividing the income proportionately among them. Segregation of the various trust shares need only be made on the books of the Trustee for accounting purpose.

(CONTINUED ON NEXT PAGE)

(CONTINUED)

O. *Compensation.* To receive reasonable compensation for the Trustee's services under this Agreement and be exonerated from and to pay all reasonable expenses and charges of the Trust.

P. *Loans to Beneficiaries.* To make loans to any trust beneficiary for the purpose of providing the beneficiary with the funds necessary to take advantage of exceptional business opportunities or to provide for the needs of the beneficiaries and their families.

Q. *Methods of Distribution.* To make payments to or for the benefit of any beneficiary (specifically including any beneficiary under any legal disability) in any of the following ways: (a) directly to the beneficiary; (b) directly for the maintenance, welfare and education of the beneficiary; (c) to the legal or natural guardian of the beneficiary; or (d) to anyone who at the time shall have custody and care of the person of the beneficiary. The Trustee shall not be obliged to see to the application of the funds so paid, but the receipt of the person to whom the funds were paid shall be full acquaintance of the Trustee.

VIII. ADDITIONAL TRUST PROVISIONS. These additional provisions shall apply regarding the Trustee.

A. *Grantor(s) as Trustee.* If at any time the Grantors or either of them shall be acting as Trustee, such Grantor(s)/ Trustee may appoint a successor trustee, to become effective immediately or upon any stated contingency, by making such designation in writing. Such designee shall become the successor Trustee upon acceptance of the terms and conditions of this Agreement

(CONTINUED ON NEXT PAGE)

B. *Successor trustee.* If at any time either Co-Trustee cannot serve because of disability (as previously defined), death, or other reason, the remaining Co-Trustee, if any, shall serve alone; otherwise (name) of XXXX, Wyoming and (name) of XXXX Minnesota are designated as successor Co-Trustees, without bond. Such designee(s) shall become the successor Trustee(s) upon acceptance of the terms and conditions of this Agreement.

C. *Resignation of Trustee.* Any Trustee may resign by giving written notice to the beneficiaries to whom income could then be distributed. Such resignation shall take effect on such date specified in the notice, but not earlier than thirty (30) days after the date of delivery of such written resignation unless an earlier effective date shall be agreed to by the income beneficiaries.

D. *Adult Beneficiary Rights.* If the trustee resigns or for any reason ceases to serve as Trustee, and if the successor Trustee(s) designated by the Grantors, if any, fail or cease to serve as Trustee, then the adult beneficiaries to whom income could then be distributed, together with the adult beneficiaries to whom principal would be distributed if the Trust were then to terminate, may by majority action in writing appoint a successor Trustee. If agreement of a majority of the appointed beneficiaries cannot be obtained within sixty (60) days, a successor Trustee shall be appointed by the court having general jurisdiction of the Trust. Any successor Trustee appointed shall have all the rights conferred upon the original Trustee and shall be bound by the provisions of this Trust.

(CONTINUED ON NEXT PAGE)

> E. *Accounting.* The Trustee shall provide an accounting to the Beneficiary (or beneficiaries) on at least an annual Basis. If a beneficiary has a "disability", the Trustee shall provide the accounting to a guardian or conservator, if any.
>
> F. *Bond.* Successor Trustees, other than those nominated in this trust, shall serve without bond.
>
> **IX. RIGHT TO DIRECT INVESTMENTS.** At the time that the trust has investments, and provided that a Grantor does not have a "disability", such Grantor may direct any Trustee to purchase, sell, or retain any trust investment.
>
> **X. REVOCATION OR AMENDMENT.** Either Grantor may revoke at any time and/or the Grantors may jointly amend this Agreement by delivering to the Trustee an appropriate written revocation or amendment, signed by the necessary Grantor or Grantors, respectively. If the Trustee consents, the powers of revocation, but not the power of amendment, may be exercised by a duly appointed attorney-in-fact for the Grantors, or either of them, for the purpose of withdrawing assets from the Trust. If the Trust is revoked, the Trustee may distribute the Trust assets to the Grantors in the same manner and amounts as the Grantors contributed the property.
>
> **XI. GOVERNING LAW.** This agreement shall be construed in accordance with the laws of the State of South Dakota.
>
> **XII. PERPETUITIES SAVING CLAUSE.** Despite any other provisions of this Agreement to the contrary, the Trust created by this Agreement shall terminate no later than 21 years after the death of the last surviving beneficiary of this Agreement who is living at the time of the death of the Surviving Grantor.

(CONTINUED ON NEXT PAGE)

(CONTINUED)

XIII. SEVERABILITY. If any portion of this Agreement shall be held to be invalid or unenforceable for any reason, the remaining provisions shall continue to be valid and enforceable. If a court finds that any provision of this Agreement is invalid or unenforceable, but that by limiting such provision it would be valid and enforceable, then such provision shall be deemed to be written, construed, and enforced as so limited.

XIV. MISCLLANEOUS PROVISIONS.

A. *Paragraph Titles and Gender.* The titles given to the paragraphs of this Trust ate inserted for reference purposes only and are not to be considered as forming a part of this Trust in interpreting its provisions. All words used in this Trust in any gender shall extend to include all genders, and any singular words shall include the plural expression, and vise versa, specifically including "child" and "children", when the context or facts so require, and any pronouns shall be taken to refer to the person or persons intended regardless of gender or number.

B. *Liability of Fiduciary.* No fiduciary who is a natural person shall, in the absence of fraudulent conduct or bad faith, be liable individually to any beneficiary of the trust estate, and the trust estate shall indemnify such natural person from any and all claims or expenses in connection with or arising out of that fiduciary's good faith actions or nonactions of the fiduciary, except for such actions or nonactions which constitute fraudulent conduct or bad faith. No successor Trustees shall be obliged to inquire into or be in any way accountable for the previous administration of the trust property.

(CONTINUED ON NEXT PAGE)

(CONTINUED)

C. Children. The names of the Grantors' children are (name), (name), and (name).

_____
Signature: John Svendson, Grantor 1

_____
Signature: Doris Svendson. Grantor 2

_____
Signature: John Svendson, Co-Trustee 1

_____
Signature: Doris Svendson, Co-Trustee 2

STATE OF SOUTH DAKOTA
COUNTY OF _____

On this 12th day of July, 2002, before me personally appeared John Svendson and Doris Svendson, to me known to be the persons described in and who executed the foregoing instrument as Grantors and Co-Trustees, and acknowledged that they executed same as their free act and deed.

_____
Notary public for the state of South Dakota
My commission expires _____

Schedule A

When John and Doris printed their trust document, a blank form was also printed. Well, it was almost blank. Except that "Schedule A" was printed at the top of the page. All living trusts have a Schedule A. This is the form on which the grantors list the assets they have transferred to their trust. There are at least two reasons for using this form, (1) the grantors will maintain an organized listing of their trust assets for their own reference (provided they keep the list current and accurate) and, (2) this Schedule A listing could be of great help to their successor trustee someday.

There are no directives on how to use Schedule A or how the grantors shall maintain it. Whatever is best for them is acceptable. They could, for example, instead of removing a sold asset from the Schedule A, they could merely line through it and note the date and reason for its removal. They could also include on Schedule A a complete listing of assets they have designated P.O.D. and T.O.D. to the trust. Again, that could be of help to the successor trustee someday. Whatever works best for the grantors is acceptable.

SOME SUGGESTIONS CONCERNING YOUR LIVING TRUST

Funding the Trust

You created the trust of your choice. Great. Lawyers will tell you that for the revocable living trust to be effective in eliminating probate, it is essential that all family assets be transferred into the trust. It's called funding the trust. What a job. Almost makes you want to abandon probate avoidance, but don't.

A lawyer friend of mine told me he transferred all of his mother's possessions to her trust. That could be a huge project. Is it really necessary to transfer all of your assets to your new trust? Transfer all real estate, stocks, bonds, bank accounts, CDs, brokerage accounts, cars, trucks, hobby collections, household goods, and garden tools? Is it really necessary to transfer your wheelbarrow and tennis racket to your trust? Of course not, it's not necessary.

One of the arguments against creating a living trust is the cost of funding it. Yes, if you have your lawyer transfer all of your assets to your trust it could be quite expensive. Some attorneys encourage clients to fund the trust themselves. Others don't give them the benefit of the doubt. They claim they must do it for them to insure it is done correctly. And why not? They charge a nice fee.

You can fund the trust yourself, and get it done right. This entails very little dollar cost, just a little paperwork, and some of your time.

Funding your trust is important but some folks take it too seriously. There's the story about the chap who signed his new trust, then immediately raced to the bank and bought a CD in his name as trustee of the trust just to make the trust "whole" and funded. That is overkill. The trust does not have to be funded immediately.

Transferring an asset into the trust is the perfect way to keep the asset from eventually going through probate. However, if you don't own assets that are best held in trust, (see chapter 16) you don't need to fund the trust. You may simply use your trust as a P.O.D. or T.O.D. beneficiary. That may be the only reason, and a very good one, for having created the trust in the first place. Attorneys don't give this reason enough emphasis. Let me do it. *Creating a trust solely for the purpose of using it as a P.O.D. or T.O.D. beneficiary is an acceptable strategy.*

Recommendations: Fund your trust when appropriate. Make it easy for yourself. Transfer to the trust only those assets that need to go there. Use a T.O.D. or P.O.D. designation to the trust for everything that has title or registration documents. A letter of assignment for everything else is optional. (See chapter 16 for suggestions on how to probate-proof each of your assets).

Bequests

Many of us want to bequeath to charity and friends. That is admirable. You state in your trust what you wish to give to whom. For example,

$15,000 to the Methodist Church, or $4,000 to the Salvation Army, $3,000 to the town library, and cash amounts to other charities or friends. But lawyers tell us not to make bequests in cash because you can't hold cash in your trust. That is technically correct. They recommend putting the cash in a bank account, and transferring the account to the trust, or designate the account P.O.D. to the charity or friend. That is another layer of paperwork no one wants.

Look, the persons you choose as successor trustees are smart and resourceful. They can devise a way of coming up with the cash and paying the bequest. For example, when real estate is sold or a brokerage account is liquidated, the cash will become available. And the bequest payments can wait until the cash is available. So even though you supposedly can't hold cash in your trust, there is no penalty for making cash bequests.

It is very unlikely the inclusion of a cash bequest would create a problem. In order for your trust or a bequest to be ruled invalid, a judge would have to see your trust and make an undesirable ruling. Plan for privacy. A judge should never see your trust. You and your successor trustees should insure that the trust remains private.

Since you created your trust and made bequests, the value of your estate can change. Not only can the value increase, but it can decrease as a result of poor investments, a recession, or medical costs in your later years. You can always change your bequests or their amount with an amendment. Or you can impose a limit now on the bequest amounts. For example, you could state that the total value of the cash bequests not exceed 15 percent of the value of your net estate less trust settlement costs. In this way you can preserve a reasonable amount for your residual beneficiaries if your estate decreases in value.

If you wish to bequest tangible personal property, you can do so in your trust. The property should be properly identified. For example, Steinway baby grand piano, serial number 1234563, or 1938 Ford pick up, serial number F38 34467, antique cherry China cupboard in the dining room at 123 State St. Peoria, IL, and 1946 Stearman airplane N47798.

However, the piano and China cupboard do not have registration documents and should not be held in the trust. They should be held in your will. Your executor can get them to the person you choose. The Ford and the Stearman do have registration documents and should be held in the trust.

What about your Dell laptop computer, the HP digital camera and your Epson printer? They have a short life expectancy and will sharply decreasing in value. Why clutter you trust or your will with these items? They can be listed with their intended recipient on a handwritten note that can be attached to your will. In fact, many people make extensive handwritten lists. They change the lists frequently whenever new items are added or old items are disposed of. And they show the lists to their successor trustees to assure complete understanding.

If you do list bequests, don't make the same bequests in you trust and your will. This could cause confusion. If you want to give $4,000 to the Salvation Army and you list the bequest in your trust and also in your will, how much is the Salvation Army supposed to get? (See Distribution Confusion in chapter 15).

The No-Contest Clause

Although challenges to the living trust are quite rare, they do occur. Anybody can challenge a trust if he or she feels the trust should be rendered invalid because of the grantor's lack of mental capacity, un-due influence during the creation of the document, or failure to have it executed properly.

Challenges for these reasons are rarely successful. If you created the trust, transferred assets into and out of the trust, and astutely managed trust property, such activity is evidence that you were competent to manage your affairs.

Nonetheless, if you think someone might challenge your trust, consider including a no-contest clause. The no-contest clause does not prevent a lawsuit. It merely discourages a beneficiary from suing. These clauses are honored in some states and partially or fully rejected in others. Consider writing a clause which reads something like this:

"Any beneficiary under this trust who sues the trust with the claim he or she should receive more than is designated for him or her, and is unsuccessful with the suit shall receive nothing."

Amending the Living Trust

While the grantor is alive, the living trust is amendable and revocable. That's why the living trust is sometimes titled

"The (Your Name) Revocable Trust" or *"The (Your Name) Revocable Living Trust."* (The name of your trust is your choice).

There are a number of reasons you may want to amend your trust—you marry, have a child, a beneficiary dies, you want to delete or add a beneficiary, you want to change share allocations, or you need to delete a successor trustee and appoint a new one. All of this can easily be done with an amendment. This is the preferred way to amend the trust. Trust writing software may provide you with a form for this purpose, or the grantor (you) can write a letter to the trustee (yourself) enumerating the changes. There is no set format for the letter, but the changes must be understandable. For example:

"delete Article VIII, paragraph B, and substitute the following paragraph.............."

You can hand write the change if you wish. (The Declaration of Independence was handwritten).

It is also possible that the software will provide you with a new *"amended and restated"* version of your original trust. You go through the interview again, make the changes, and then print the new version.

Date and sign the document. Witnesses are not required. But you must sign in front of a notary public, and have the document notarized. Attach the amendment to your trust. It is suggested you note on the first page of the trust that an amendment of (date) exists. Review the amendment with your successor trustee to insure complete understanding.

Revoking Your Living Trust

There is very little reason to revoke your trust. Almost everything can be done with an amendment. If the trust is in such bad shape you don't feel you can amend it, then create a new trust and transfer the assets from the problem trust to the new one. Otherwise you have to transfer everything out of the trust and into your name. Then you won't avoid probate for that property. In either event this is another round of paperwork similar to the paperwork involved in transferring property to the trust the first time. The amendment sounds better and better.

Once you have transferred everything out of a trust, the trust becomes unfunded. But the trust doesn't go away. If you really want to revoke it, you have to fill out another form, a Revocation of Trust. But why bother? The trust does no damage, and maybe you will want to use it again later. For example, you are in your second marriage. You brought with you from you first marriage separate property, a 1939 Chevy, which you eventually want to go to your son. Why not try one more time to amend the problem trust just so it can hold the Chevy, and nothing else? Otherwise create a new trust. Yes, now you have two (or more) living trusts, a joint living trust with your current wife, and a single living trust holding an unrestored 1939 Chevrolet. You can have as many revocable living trusts as you want.

CHAPTER NINE

THE AB TRUST

WHEN A PERSON DIES his estate is subject to the Federal Estate Tax, more popularly known as the death tax. Every estate valued in excess of the estate tax threshold may be subject to the death tax. If you die in 2018, the amount of your estate in excess of $11.2 million is taxed at the rate of 40%.

The AB trust is a living trust available to married couples only. It reduces or eliminates federal estate taxes—and in some cases state taxes also—for "large" estates. "Large" can't be defined because the laws keep changing and the amounts exempt from taxation keep changing. Each person in a marriage is permitted the $11.2 million exemption. If you are married, you might consider creating an AB trust if your estate might someday be subject to the tax. It could save your estate significant tax.

Marriage

Since the AB Trust is available to married couples only, let's talk about marriage. In most states it is necessary to file papers with the county clerk and have a marriage ceremony performed by an authorized individual in order to be considered married. However, a few states honor what is known as "common law marriage." In those states opposite sex couples may be considered married and eligible to create an AB trust if they have lived together for a certain period of time and intended to be husband and wife. You can make an internet search for common-law marriage laws in your state to determine your eligibility for the AB trust. Or consult an attorney.

The federal government also recognizes same-sex marriage. Same-sex couples should determine if the AB trust could benefit them.

The Marital Deduction

At any time, any married person can pass any amount of his or her estate—no matter how large—to his or her spouse without any tax at all. And the first spouse to die can leave all of his or her estate to the surviving spouse with no tax. This practice is for married couples only and is known as the marital deduction. The marital deduction really acts like a gift and estate tax exemption.

Under the joint living trust the deceased spouse's property not scheduled to be given to beneficiaries transfers to the surviving spouse. That is a marital deduction. Under the AB Trust there is no marital deduction; the surviving spouse must establish Trust A for the deceased's property and Trust B for the survivor's property.

Joe and Clara Create an AB Trust

The AB trust reduces or eliminates estate taxes by establishing, at the time of death of the first spouse, a life estate the surviving spouse. (See life estate in chapter 3). The survivor doesn't own the life estate property but receives income from it and has the right to spend the principal for his or her health care, support, and maintenance as necessary to maintain the survivor's normal and accustomed lifestyle.

The prevailing opinion is that most married couples don't have to consider an AB trust because less that 0.2% of Americans have estates large enough to end up owing the tax. But those who benefit from the AB trust not only avoid probate, they also save on death taxes.

Joe and Clara owned shared property worth $18 million held in their trust. When Joe dies, the AB trust property owned by Joe and Clara will divide into two trusts. Trust A, called the bypass or family trust, will contain all of Joe's separate property not designated to be given away to beneficiaries after his death, and half of the shared AB trust property. Trust A becomes the irrevocable life estate trust. Trust B, known as the survivor's trust or marital trust, will contain all of Clara's separate property and the other half of the AB trust shared property. Trust B remains revocable. Clara becomes the trustee for both trusts. Clara should employ an attorney to establish these trusts.

The amount placed in Trust A will be half of the estate. ($9 million). Clara's Trust B, the marital trust, will also be funded with $9 million. If Clara were to die while the federal estate tax exemption is $11.2 million, both Trust A and Trust B would be exempt from taxation, and the assets would pass to the beneficiaries, usually the children, free of tax.

If Joe and Clara had not created an AB trust, the $18 million estate of the surviving spouse, Clara, could be subjected to a huge tax when she dies. At the 2018 rate of 40%, the $6.8 million in excess of the federal estate tax threshold would result in a tax of $2.72 million. That is a grim thought.

The AB trust is also known by other names. It is often called a "credit shelter trust," "marital life estate trust," "spousal bypass trust, "and the "exemption trust." It does a fine job in saving estate taxes for married couples. If you or your spouse were to die, and the survivor's estate might exceed the federal estate tax exemption, then you should consider creating an AB trust.

THE AB DISCLAIMER TRUST

There is a better option than the AB Trust. It is the AB Disclaimer Trust. It is also known as the AB Trust with a Disclaimer Clause. If a married couple has an estate not subject to estate tax, but think they may be subject to estate taxes sometime in the future, and they don't know what the federal estate tax exemption will be in 10 or 15 years (nobody knows), and they don't want to be required to split their estate into trust A and trust B unless a split would benefit them, they can eliminate these concerns with a AB Disclaimer trust.

A young couple in our community won a lottery. The amount did not exceed the estate tax exemption limit, but Bill and Jen were frugal and foresaw that their fortune may gain value over time, and they wanted to avoid taxes. They needed help. I suggested an AB disclaimer trust.

Bill and Jen decided the AB disclaimer trust would be perfect. Their declaration of trust is called the William (last name) and Jennifer (last name) Living Trust. The trust lists the names of the grantors, the trustees, the successor trustees, and the final beneficiaries. The document does not state that it is an AB trust or AB disclaimer trust.

The AB trust dictates that after the death of the first spouse to die the deceased spouse's assets pass to the surviving spouse and are to be placed in Trust B. The following paragraph is the disclaimer clause and makes that placement optional:

> *"The surviving spouse has the authority to disclaim any trust assets left to him or her by the deceased spouse. The surviving spouse is not required to disclaim any of these trust assets. If the surviving spouse chooses to disclaim property, he or she shall do so within nine months after the deceased spouse's death. Any disclaimed property shall be called the "Bypass Trust Share," and shall be held and administered in Trust A. If the surviving spouse does not disclaim any assets left to him or her by the deceased spouse's trust, the trustee shall not establish Trust A."*

After the death of the first spouse to die the survivor should consult financial advisors and estate planning attorneys to make the decision whether to disclaim or accept the marital deduction. If the survivor is in poor health, it might be necessary to make that decision soon. Death of the second grantor before Trust A is established could cause a tax liability that could have been avoided with early action.

If the survivor decides to disclaim the assets of the deceased spouse, trusts A and B will be created. If the survivor does nothing, A and B are not created and the trust can be administered as though it were a basic joint living trust.

The decision to create an AB trust is important. The AB Disclaimer Trust is a very attractive option.

My recommendation: If there is a remote chance that you would benefit from an AB trust, create an AB trust with a disclaimer clause.

My additional recommendation: Married couples with estates that may exceed the federal estate tax exemption limit very likely have complicated estates. They should consult an estate tax attorney. Reread this chapter before that visit.

CHAPTER TEN

HOW DO I GET A LIVING TRUST?
AND
HOW MUCH WILL IT COST?

YOU HAVE DECIDED you need a revocable living trust. Good decision. We all need a living trust for any number of reasons. But what is it going to cost, and where do we get the best deal?

Everyone has told us it's too expensive. Your family lawyer may have told you that probate is cheaper and easier. Let's prove them all wrong.

There are five ways you can get your living trust.

1. Hire an attorney or law firm to prepare the trust and other estate planning documents.
2. The Trust Mill
3. Create you own documents online.
4. Buy the living trust software and create the document on your computer.
5. Buy a living trust form kit and fill in the blanks.

Which is best? I'll tell you right now the least expensive, safest, and most private way to create your living trust is at home on your computer. Nonetheless, let's look at all the possibilities.

HIRE AN ATTORNEY

You could start with your family attorney. However, I believe most family attorneys prefer to someday settle your estate under probate later rather than create a living trust for you now. Probate will be a much larger financial gain for the attorney. Lawyers make a ton of money taking clients estates through probate. If he tells you a will is all you need, or that "probate is simple in this state" you will immediately know where he stands on the issue. Sure, probate might be simple where you live, but why subject your heirs to the cost and inconvenience of probate? When you realize your attorney is not enthusiastic about the job, you should search elsewhere.

An attorney will charge you more to create a living trust than to make a will because the legal industry has led us all to believe the trust is more complex and difficult to write. It is not. It is common to charge you for 10 hours of work to create a trust and a pour-over will. At $150 per hour you're looking at $1,500 or more. Separately, they may charge $1,000 for the trust and $500 for the will. Her fee may not include transferring assets to the trust. And there may be additional charges for the other documents you need.

During the first visit your attorney will ask a series of questions: the names of your chosen beneficiaries, how much each beneficiary will receive, and any special bequests to charity or others you wish to make. And he will need the names and addresses of the successor trustees. This session may take one hour. If he is conscientious, he will take some extra time to give you some legal advice and explain the other documents you need, how they will be of benefit to your beneficiaries, and how they will save money for your estate and your heirs. (See the Five Important Documents in the appendix).

After the interview he will hand your answers to a paralegal or a low level clerk who will enter the information into a computer program, and presto, in another hour your living trust and pour-over will is ready to print. Days or perhaps weeks later you will visit with the attorney again to insure the documents are as you want them. Any changes would take only a few minutes. It is hard to believe the whole process would take 10 hours of attorney time, but who are you to know?

YIELD TO THE TRUST MILL

There is another way to hire an attorney to create your living trust. It's the high-pressure trust mill. You may receive an invitation to attend a seminar emphasizing estate planning and living trust creation. These seminars are conducted by law firms which specializes in living trusts. If you get suckered in and they produce documents for you, there is no guarantee their products will protect all of your assets from probate and reduce taxes as they promise. You may not get instructions on how to probate-proof assets that they fail to protect from probate. I attended a trust mill seminar recently. The salesman knew his material and delivered a terrific sales pitch. Most of what he said was true except for his contention that there was no way you could create your own trust and other documents yourself.

The cost for a living trust, last will and testament, and durable power of attorney was $3750, but if you signed up that afternoon you would get his "trust package" for a reduced price of $3250. This service included quitclaim deeds for a maximum two in-state real properties. I guess if you owned real estate in another state you were on your own.

The after-seminar open-faced turkey sandwich was horrible.

Attend a seminar and see what you can learn. But read this book again before you sign up with the trust mill. And read below to see what else is available for creating your living trust and the other documents you should have.

CREATE YOUR TRUST ONLINE

You don't have to hire a lawyer to create a valid living trust. You can do it online. Costs vary but are generally reasonable. They are definitely less than a lawyer would charge. Do an online search for "living trust online." There are an ample number of sites to explore. Legalzoom. com is just one example. The sites are web based so you can use any computer.

Log on to the website and select the document you wish to create. Then answer the all the questions, review the finished document, and make payment. In a few days your documents will arrive by mail.

My objection to creating your documents online is that you leave your personal data in cyberspace, in the cloud, and on some far-away server.

CREATE THE LIVING TRUST
ON YOUR COMPUTER

Buy the living trust software and create the living trust on your computer. When you buy will and trust writing software, you own it and get to use it repeatedly to create documents for family and friends. And the private information is kept private on your computer. It doesn't end up on the server of some distant website.

Software is available from many sources. A Google search for "living trust software" will provide a sizable list of what is available. The costs are reasonable.

The largest source for will and trust writing software is Nolo Press (Nolo.com). I prefer Nolo's "Make Your Own Living Trust" by Denis Clifford. Included are the Basic Trust for the Individual, the Shared Living Trust, and the AB Disclaimer Trust. The software can be ordered as eBook alone or soft cover book and eBook. The cost is less that $50. Of course you will be able to use this trust writing software repeatedly to help parents, and friends and neighbors probate-proof their estates.

As I write a free sample Declaration of Trust for an individual is available on the Nolo.com website. The sample says it conforms to Arizona law. In reality the trust created using this sample will be valid in all 50 states (with the possible exception of Louisiana owning to Napoleonic law). I copied and pasted this trust into a Word document and used it repeatedly to create individual and joint trusts. Simply change the names of the grantor(s), trustee(s), and beneficiaries. Presto, a free living trust. Zero cost. Perfect.

Many of you will want to take your new trust to a lawyer for review. I recommend against that. Most lawyers prefer probate cases and don't want to approve a trust document they didn't prepare.

BUY INDIVIDUAL FORMS OR FORM KITS

The fifth way to get the documents you need is to search for blank forms or form kits. What's available can be found by making Google searches for "living trust forms" or "living trust kits."

Downloaded blank forms, and forms included in form kits are frequently a one-size-fits-all solution to a serious matter. The result may be inferior product when filled out by a customer with limited legal knowledge and insufficient guidance on how to properly complete the document.

The laws concerning living trusts differ slightly from state to state. The trust you create using fill-in forms may not comply with all the requirements of your state. Books and kits of legal forms may be useful for such needs as bills of sale, petitions to change your name, real estate sales agreement, and promissory notes. But when it comes to the living trust, they may be of poor quality and lack important provisions.

MAKE A DECISION

You get the biggest bang for the buck buying professional software and creating the living trust and other documents yourself. Millions of Americans prepare their taxes using TurboTax. Because of the complexity of the tax code, it is almost impossible to complete your annual income tax return without software help or without paying a tax preparer who couldn't care less how much he saves you. You know the old adage, "If you want it done right, do it yourself." Buy the living trust and will writing software and create professional estate planning documents yourself.

There are definite advantages if you do it yourself. You don't share your private information with an attorney who doesn't have his heart in the project or with trust mill salesmen who couldn't care less about your personal situation. And you don't leave your private information and copies of your completed documents on the server of some far-away website.

When you buy the software and create the documents on your own computer, you do so with complete privacy. The finished document is just as professional as that your lawyer would provide you. You can change the document and print it again if you don't like the first one. In fact, if you can't decide whether you want a Joint Living Trust or an AB Trust, create both and then choose.

The software is yours to keep. Share it with your kids or parents so they can produce their living trusts, wills, powers of attorney, and a myriad of other documents.

The high cost myth has been blown away. If you can create your living trust and all the other necessary documents for a lot less that 100 bucks (and you can), cost is no excuse for not having a trust. Go for it. Get one.

WILL YOUR LIVING TRUST BE VALID?

You buy trust writing software and create you revocable living trust. You share it with your successor trustee but no one else. You keep it private. Later the laws in your state change but your trust remains valid. You are grandfathered in. You move to another state and your trust remains valid. You move overseas and your trust remains valid. No matter where you are when you die, your revocable living trust remains valid and your estate will avoid probate.

THE ABSTRACT OF TRUST

When you transfer property to your trust, a bank or other institutions will ask for a copy of your trust. Present them instead with an Abstract of Trust (also called a Certificate of Trust). This abstract is proof that the trust exists. The abstract is easy to prepare. It should include only those pages of the trust which list the names of the grantor(s) and the trustee(s), and the powers of the trustees, and a copy of the trust signature page.

CHAPTER ELEVEN

THE THREE-TRUST FAMILY

ALAN AND JANE, A MARRIED COUPLE, decided to create a trust to probate-proof their estate. This was the second marriage for each. Alan had
two adult sons, Mark and Charles. Jane had an adult son, Jeff, and a
daughter, Jennifer.

Alan and Jane bought trust writing software and decided on a joint
living trust. After they listed themselves as grantors and trustees the
program asked what assets they intended to hold in the trust, who
owned each asset, and who will be the final beneficiary for each asset.

They owned their home together, and each owned separate property from their first marriages. All the assets were fed into the computer,
who owned them, and who would inherit them. Their compiled list is
on the next page.

They experienced problems compiling a list of trust assets:

- Listing an item on a trust form does not make it a trust asset.
  You have to take action to transfer each item to the trust.

- Jane never liked the Hupmobile and didn't want to serve as the
  trustee to transfer the car to Mark if Alan dies before she does.

- Property with no title or registration document, such as the
  John Deere tractor, the Van Gogh painting, the Spode China,
  and the sterling silver bowl, does not need to be transferred to

Asset	Owner	Final Beneficiary
Home at 234 Aspen	Alan and Jane	Four Children
2001 Jeep	Alan and Jane	Four Children
2007 Honda Accord	Alan and Jane	Four Children
Edward Jones account	Alan and Jane	Four Children
Safe Deposit Box	Alan and Jane	Four Children
1938 Hupmobile	Alan	Mark
1955 Studebaker	Alan	Charles
Scottrade account	Alan	Mark and Charles
1964 Piper Tripacer	Alan	Mark and Charles
John Deere 70 Diesel	Alan	Mark and Charles
Lakefront Property	Jane	Jeff and Jennifer
Brokerage account	Jane	Jeff and Jennifer
Van Gogh painting	Jane	Jeff
Spode China	Jane	Jennifer
Sterling Silver bowl	Jane	Sister Beth

the trust. If you want to hold tangible personal property in a trust, you can do so on an Assignment of Property form (samples available online) or by writing a Letter of Assignment. (A sample Letter of Assignment is in the appendix). Sign the form and keep it with your trust document.

- The safe deposit box is not a trust asset. Alan and Jane do not own the safe deposit box. The bank owns the box. The Alan and Jane lease the box and own the contents. They have access to the contents at any time.

- Over time the list of assets will be out of date.

Alan and Jane printed their joint living trust. All the assets were listed on schedules A, B, or C. Schedule A listed all the property they owned together. Schedule B listed all of Alan's separate property, and Schedule C listed Jane's separate property.

They read the trust and its schedules. They realized the lists would change. Then Jane said, "Alan, when you pass away, I will grieve, and I would rather not serve as trustee for your property. Why don't you create your own individual trust and name Mark as successor trustee and Charles as alternate successor trustee? And I will create an individual living trust for my stuff."

Alan and Jane agreed to three trusts. They became a three-trust family. For their shared property they chose an AB Disclaimer Trust. They listed no property in the trust document. They wrote a quitclaim deed transferring their home to their AB Disclaimer trust. They went to the DMV with the titles to the Jeep and Honda and titled them to themselves as trustee of the Alan and Jane AB Disclaimer Trust. Mark and Jeff were successor co-trustees. They went to the Edward Jones brokerage office and signed paperwork designating their account T.O.D. to the their trust. When an asset was moved to the trust, an entry was made on schedule A.

Alan and Jane also created individual trusts. Again, they made no specific listing of property within the trusts. When they transferred property to their individual trusts, they made a handwritten listing of the property on the specific Schedule A for that trust.

Alan and Jane selected different names for their trusts to avoid confusion. Alan named his trust the Alan (last name) Automobile Trust. Jane called her trust the Jane (last name) Lakefront Trust.

Since Alan and Jane both have children from their first marriages they should create a Life Estate Trust which, after the death of the first spouse to die, allow the surviving spouse to remain in their home until that spouse dies. This will avoid the need to sell the house to satisfy the children's request for their inheritance. (I recommend an attorney prepare this trust).

Is it sensible to have three trusts? Sure, you can have as many as you want. If it makes life easier—and it certainly did in the case of Alan and Jane—create three, or more.

You won't find the three trust concept advocated in many estate planning manual, but it is a viable solution worth considering.

CONSIDER THESE TRUSTS

There are a number of trusts you may want to consider in addition to the living trust. Here are just a few:

Charitable Lead Trust
Charitable Remainder Trust
Generation - Skipping Trusts (GSTT Trusts)
Grantor Retained Interest Trusts: GRATs, GRUTs, and GRITs
Life Insurance Trusts
Testamentary trusts (Trusts established by your will)
Business Trusts

Some of these trusts are revocable during the grantor's lifetime. Some are irrevocable. They have different objectives. Many will avoid probate for the trust assets. Some are established to reduce the size of the estate and thus reduce taxes.

You can read about these trusts in your favorite estate-planning book. Consult an attorney to see if any are right for you.

AVOID THESE TRUSTS

There are con men who argue that you can use trusts to avoid or eliminate income taxes. They promote a whole menagerie of domestic and offshore "constitutional" trusts, "pure" trusts, "equipment" trusts, "common law trust organizations" (COLATOS), and "foreign common law trust organizations" (FORCOLATOS), and the like. Use of these trusts violates the IRS tax code. And if you try to fight the IRS, you will lose.

The use of these questionable trusts is dangerous. The IRS published a basic warning in IRS Publication 2193, "Too Good to be True Trusts". You can view this publication online. It is in PDF form. Google IRS Publication 2193.

Be forewarned. Avoid trusts that will cause you trouble.

CHAPTER TWELVE

THE LAST WILL AND TESTAMENT

IT IS CALLED THE LAST WILL AND TESTAMENT because it is the most recent and supersedes all your previous wills and amendments known as codicils.

The purpose of the will is to choose who gets your property after you die. This distribution applies only to the property held in the will, not to property you have removed from your will through the use of a will substitute such as joint ownership (Chapter 5), beneficiary designation (Chapter 6), or transfer to your living trust (Chapter 7). In your will you name the executor of your estate (executrix in the case of the female executor, but the term executor generally applies to both genders now). The executor executes the will after your death and settles the estate. In some states your executor is known as your personal representative. Same job, different label.

The maker of the will is known as the testator.

REASONS FOR MAKING A WILL

Avoid Intestacy — Your will keeps the government from deciding who gets your stuff. If you have a will, you are considered testate. If you fail to make a will you are considered intestate. If you are intestate and your family has to hire a lawyer or go to probate court for help in settling your estate, the court will choose your beneficiaries according to state law and appoint an administrator to settle the estate. None of these people, (the administrator or the beneficiaries), may be the folks you would have chosen. That is an excellent reason for making a will.

Choose Your Executor — When you make a Last Will and Testament, you get to choose the executor of your estate. A spouse, adult children or other trusted person is usually chosen. Sometimes co-executors are chosen, and this is fine if these persons get along well. An alternate executor should also be chosen in the event the primary executor cannot serve. The chosen executor does not have to reside in the state in which you reside. However, if the probate judge must appoint an administrator (in the case of intestacy), he or she will be a local resident and US citizen.

The executor/administrator does not have to have to be a financial genius or legal expert, but common sense and life experience are desirable. The executor should be capable and competent, loyal, and trustworthy. Personal integrity is essential. He or she should be smart enough to seek the advice of experts when needed.

The same criteria should be used when selecting the successor trustee of your living trust. To avoid conflicts, your executor and successor trustee should be the same person.

You should discuss your estate with your chosen executor(s). Your executors must be assured that all possible steps have been taken to prevent probate. Surely you want to spare them the aggravation and hassle of probate.

You should also provide them with copies of your Will, Living Trust, Living Will, Durable Power of Attorney for Finance, and Power of Attorney for Health Care. These are documents all estates should have; they are listed in more detail in the appendix. A good software program should provide all of these documents, or they can be found on the internet.

There may be reasons your first choice for executor may not wish to serve. Known animosity or family feuding between beneficiaries may be one reason. Suspicion that someone left out may contest the will could be another reason. Large debts owed creditors of the estate could pose a severe problem. These matters should be resolved before you ask anyone to serve as your executor.

Select Guardians for Your Children — In your will you select the person or persons who shall become the guardians of your minor children and manage the property or money that you leave to your children. You can't designate guardians in your trust; it's done in your will. Normally a surviving spouse will be appointed as guardian after your death. Whether single or married, an alternate guardian is usually selected in your will to serve in the event that you and your spouse suffer simultaneous death or your first named guardian fails to survive you.

Even though you insulate your estate from probate—by establishing for yourself a non-probate estate—your executor might have to present your will to the probate court so that the guardian you named can be appointed by the court.

Wills presented to the court for any reason usually become public documents. Anyone can view the will. When this happens the names of beneficiaries you list in the will and the assets they are to receive become public information. You may object to this—and rightly so. Fortunately there is a remedy. Do not name individuals as beneficiaries in your will. Do that in your living trust instead. The living trust remains a private document. In your will name your living trust as the beneficiary and bequeath your assets to the living trust. This is known as a pour-over will. If you have a non-probate estate, your will won't be filed for probate and become public.

Select a Manager to Manage Property Left to Children — This selection must be made in your will. It cannot be made in your trust. The selection of property manager could be different than the selection of guardian.

HOLD THE NON-PROBATE PROPERTY
IN YOUR WILL

You don't have to transfer all of your assets to your living trust. Your will is where you can safely hold non-probate property. This is property that can pass to beneficiaries without probate. The assets you can safely hold in your will are tangible personal property without title or registration papers. Examples are household goods, furniture (even antiques), paintings (even fine art), tools, toys, hobby collections, hardware, coins, fishing equipment, even wheelbarrows and tennis rackets. If you make a pour-over will (described below), the tangible personal property will pour-over to the trust after you death and then go to the trust beneficiaries.

The will is a catchall for property you forgot to move to your living trust or designate a beneficiary to receive. It is also a catchall for recently acquired property such as your last pay check or social security payment. Your appointed executor can take necessary action to move these assets to you trust or distribute them to your beneficiaries.

DO YOU REALLY NEED A WILL?

Yes, all attorneys suggest that even though you create a living trust you still need a will. This is where you specify who gets the assets left in your will, either on purpose or by accident, when you forgot to move them to your trust. But if your affairs are very simple and all you assets are designated for automatic pay-on-death transfer to a beneficiary after you die, you may get by without a will. For example, if you are a widow, you rent your home, and all your assets such as bank accounts, certificates of deposit, brokerage accounts are set up to pay on-death to your daughter, your only child, you probably don't need a will. If your affairs are slightly more complicated and you would like to bequeath to a charity or to a longtime friend, or you have more than one beneficiary, you need a will. Don't take a chance. Make a will.

Yes, your family would appreciate a will to work from. In fact, they should insist that you make one. It is a simple task.

I have a non-probate estate. But I also have a will. A sample holographic will is in the appendix. It's a pour-over will. The will assets pour over into the trust. (See the various types of wills below).

Some people don't make a will because they don't think its important, they don't have family to give their property to, or they would rather the next generation worry about it. Some want the court to solve the matter. That's their choice.

Incidentally, you may have noticed that the correct terminology is you "create" a trust and "make" a will. Just so you know.

WHICH TYPE OF WILL IS RIGHT FOR YOU?

Basic or Simple Will — A will that provides for the straightforward distribution of assets from an uncomplicated estate to final beneficiaries is known as a simple will. It can serve as a back up for a living trust. If you bequeath all your will assets to your living trust, the simple will becomes a pour-over will.

The Joint Will — The joint will is also known as the marital will. If a married couple can agree on what they want done with their property, they can make a joint will. This is not a good idea because the survivor can't change the will and in most cases can't revoke it. The property could be tied up for years. It is much better for each spouse to make his or her own will. Most lawyers discourage the joint will.

The Pour-Over Will — Most estate planning attorneys recommend a pour-over will (assuming you create a trust). This will takes all property left in your will at the time of your death, including recently acquired property, and transfers it to your living trust. Again, the assets must be non-probate assets. They must be able to pass to your beneficiaries without going through probate. The document may not be titled a pour-over will, but it becomes one when you bequeath of all your will assets to your living trust. Spouses usually leave most of their property to their surviving spouse. If their spouse predeceases them, then the property will transfer as a bequest to the living trust. The pour-over will is not difficult to make. Will writing software easily leads you through the process.

Living Will — The living will is not a will. It is an Advanced Health Care Directive. It provides specific directions about the medical treatment you wish to have followed if someday you cannot speak for yourself. It appoints someone to make these decisions for you.

Everyone needs a living will. The trust and will writing software should provide you with a living will. Many communities have living will forms available at the local hospital.

The Oral Will — Oral Wills derive from a time when soldiers and sailors dying of wounds in the heat of battle made an oral Last Will and Testament. These wills may have been accepted at one time, but not anymore. If you tell your daughter, "When I die everything I have becomes yours," you have just created an oral will. But anyone who creates such a will probably hasn't taken the trouble to avoid probate. What's more, the will can't be proven and oral wills are not accepted in most states. Your estate will likely be headed for probate.

The Holographic Will — The holographic will is written entirely in the handwriting of the testator. It must state what the testator intends to do with his property. The testator must sign it, but the signature does not need to be witnessed or notarized. If there is a challenge (rare), it may be necessary to get a handwriting expert to prove the will is in the decedents handwriting. But handwriting is easy to prove.

About half the states accept holographic wills. To find out if your state accepts holographic wills, Google "(your state) holographic will," or call the Register of Wills at your county courthouse and ask if holographic wills are accepted.

A sample holographic will is in the appendix. This sample holographic will is also a pour-over will.

SHOULD YOU PREPARE A WILL FOR EASY PROBATE?

This question is asked in some estate planning manuals. It is a ridiculous question. The answer of course is *No*. You don't plan a will for any probate, hard or easy. Your will should contain only non-probate property which your executor can distribute to beneficiaries privately and free of probate. When you create a non-probate estate, you avoid probate.

SIGNING THE WILL

Usually two witnesses, and in some states three witnesses, must be present when you sign your will and they must sign as witnesses. And the witnesses must be adults and usually must not be beneficiaries of your will. They do not have to sign in front of a notary public. But attorneys recommend that these witnesses be local people and younger than you so that later they will still be alive and available to testify before the probate court that the witness signatures are indeed theirs. That sounds like fun.

It is unlikely that your Last Will and Testament will ever have to be submitted to the probate court for signature verification. In most cases your signature, witnessed by a notary, and your witness signatures without a notarization will do just fine. However, if the Court wants to prove your will 20 years from now, the witnesses may be living in another state or have died. Proof could be difficult and time consuming. As a remedy, will writing software should provide you with a self-proving affidavit. The form prints automatically when you print your will. If you and your witnesses sign the will and the self-proving affidavit in front of a notary, and the notary signs also, your will becomes self-proving, and the witnesses will not have to appear in court in order in order to affirm the validity of the will. Yes, it's inconvenient. Nonetheless, if you think it is necessary, drag your witnesses before a notary, have everybody sign, and then go out for pizza.

There is no need to sign more than one copy of the will. If you want to make copies to give to your executor or family members, give them unsigned copies. When you later write a new will, you won't feel compelled to collect copies of the old will. A new will supersedes all previous wills and codicils.

SIGNING THE HOLOGRAPHIC WILL

If your state accepts holographic wills, you have an easy out. Find a sample pour-over will that you like (mine is in the appendix). Make the will in your own handwriting. A pour-over will is usually just one page in length, so it is not a big project. Also explain in a short sentence that this is your holographic will and request its acceptance. Then sign and date the will. There is no need to sign before a notary. What could be easier?

Since legible penmanship has been in a steady decline since the 1930s, few people can read anyone's handwriting. In fact, many of us can't read our own handwriting. If your handwriting is difficult to read attach your holographic will to a printed version to help others decipher what you wrote.

CHANGING YOUR WILL

A will is changeable and revocable while you live. If you want to change your will you can write an amendment known as a codicil, but it is easier to crank up the will writing software and make a new will. Your new will replaces all previous wills. If you want to revoke your will, simply write a new one. That is the best way to have a current will.

THE WASHINGTON SUPERWILL

Your will does not normally control assets outside your will, but the government of the State of Washington experienced a burst of incredible wisdom and created what is called the Washington Superwill Provision. The Washington Superwill Provision allows the testator, when making a new will, to either knowingly or unknowingly change the beneficiary designation for assets already designated P.O.D., and even change the beneficiary designations for assets held in a living trust. What a great way to mess up a perfectly good estate plan. Before you make a new will in Washington, it would be wise to consult an attorney.

CHAPTER THIRTEEN

CHECKING ACCOUNTS

THERE ARE FOUR CHECKING accounts you need to know about.

1. The Estate Checking Account
2. The Checking Account for Trust Settlement
3. The Convenience Checking Account
4. The Trust Account

THE ESTATE CHECKING ACCOUNT

The Estate Checking Account is a bank account used by the estate's executor to collect the deceased's assets, pay the estate's bills, and settle the probate estate. To open the account the executor chooses a bank, preferable the deceased's bank, but it can be any bank. I suggest opening the account in the state where the deceased lived. If the account is opened in another state, taxes could be due in two states.

The banker will ask for three documents: a death certificate, Letters Testamentary from the probate court appointing the executor, and the executor's personal identification. The banker will also ask for the Employee Identification Number (EIN). If the executor doesn't have the EIN, the account can't be opened until one is obtained.

The EIN will be used only if the estate, while being settled, earns enough income to require filing a tax return. This is rare, but nonetheless the EIN is required. To obtain the EIN, go online to IRS.gov, select Forms and Pubs, keep searching for the truly imaginative IRS Form SS-4, Application for Employee Identification Number. You are not going to be an employer, of course, but this is the form you need. You can also go to the Social Security Office or the Post Office for Form SS-4.

Call the phone number of on the back of the form and get the EIN right away, or fill out the form and mail it to the IRS and get the number in about four weeks.

The banker should provide some checks so that the executor, after making deposits, can begin paying bills.

THE CHECKING ACCOUNT FOR TRUST SETTLEMENT

When you have a living trust and a non-probate estate, your successor trustee will skip the trip to the probate court to obtain Letters Testamentary. That is a big relief.

At the bank the successor trustee will present a death certificate, an Abstract of Trust, her personal identification, and you guessed it, an EIN. This isn't terribly burdensome. She will get the checking account she needs to settle the trust.

In most cases the trust can be settled quickly and the EIN will not be used. If the trust assets must be managed for some time, and the trust earns income, taxes may be due. In that case I advise getting help from a CPA or tax attorney.

Please note that the successor trustee will not be settling an estate. The non-probate estate ceased upon the death of the last grantor to die. Legally there is no estate to settle. The successor trustee (who is now the new trustee) settles the *trust*.

A Better Idea

First, probate-proof your estate. Then take your successor trustee(s) (your children) with you to the bank and add their names to your checking account as joint tenants with the right of survivorship (JT-WROS). The end beneficiaries must understand that this is done not to gift the value of half of your account to the new joint tenants, but to have them in place to ultimately serve as trustees and settle your trust. No EIN is required.

The account registration doesn't need to be changed. Also, there is no need to change the printing on your checks. Your name and address, or whatever you have used in the past, will be fine. If fact, what you have imprinted on your checks is unimportant to the banker or the banking system, and you absolutely don't have to print your successor trustee's name on the checks.

The account is now ready for use when that time comes to settle your trust. In the meantime, the account can be used as a Convenience Checking Account when the grantor needs help. (See Convenience Checking Account below).

The bank doesn't need to be informed when the primary account holder dies. Checks written to the deceased grantor will be deposited into the account. Payments written in favor of the trustee of the trust will likewise be deposited into the account because he or she is a joint tenant. The successor trustee (the new trustee) can quickly and privately settle the trust.

All deposits and payments should be recorded in a check register. The check register becomes a complete record of all financial transactions completed to settle the trust. Good records answer a lot of questions and discourage protests by dissatisfied beneficiaries or others.

Note: This recommendation should appear in every estate planning manual, but it does not. The Estate Checking Account, its existence, and its use are rarely mentioned. Even less is mentioned about the account used by the trustee to settle the trust. I strongly recommend the account be established now. Add the name of your successor trustee to your account now. Your successor trustee will be mighty glad you did.

THE CONVENIENCE CHECKING ACCOUNT

Many elderly persons need help managing their financial affairs. They commonly add a son, daughter, or other trustworthy relative to their checking account as an additional owner. If you add your successor trustee(s), the account can ultimately be used to settle your trust. The bank staff usually sets up the account as a joint tenancy with right of survivorship. The new joint tenant is frequently known as the convenience owner. The convenience owner collects the funds and pays the bills anytime the primary owner needs help. This system is quite acceptable and works very well. No, you don't have to print your convenience owner's name on your checks.

As an alternative to adding a convenience owner to your checking account some states let depositors name one or more "agents" who have the right to make deposits, make withdrawals, and write checks on the depositor's behalf. These agents have no right to the money. If you have established an account like this you will need to designate the account P.O.D. to your trust. You don't want this account to become a probate asset. Ask your banker what is available and customary where you bank.

There Could Be Concerns When Adding A Convenience Owner

The convenience owner must be honest, responsible, and prepared to willingly carry out your wishes, verbal and written. This is not a problem if you select the right person.

Joint tenancy is generally reachable by creditors of any joint tenant, regardless of who originally owned or funded the account. If your convenience owner or the owner added to your account loses a lawsuit, your account could be in jeopardy. But if you maintain a low account balance, creditors will be discouraged from going after the account.

When you add a new owner, that transfer into joint tenancy may be a taxable gift. The new owner theoretically now owns his prorated share of the account. At least that is what our friendly IRS will tell you. If the convenience owner withdrawals from the account for his or her own use an amount which exceeds the annual tax-free amount for that year, a gift tax return, IRS Form 709, is supposed to be filed. That is a nasty form. Avoid it. Making large withdrawals or payments only for the benefit of the primary owner avoids this.

Some Attorneys Object

Some estate planning attorneys object to adding a convenience owner to your checking account. They believe it is safer to give your trusted person the power of attorney instead. This person, known as an attorney-in-fact, can act on your behalf under all the conditions you specify, banking included. Yes, you need to grant a power of attorney. That is one of the five documents I recommend everyone should create. (The list of the five important documents is in the appendix).

Any power of attorney you grant terminates upon your death.

You need a convenience owner as a joint tenant of your checking account. That joint owner (your successor trustee) can use the account to settle your trust.

Final Disposition for the Checking Account

The last surviving joint tenant becomes the owner of a joint account by law. It is advisable to inform your successor trustee and your beneficiaries of your desire to have the final balance of your account become part of your pour-over will. I recently included the following statement in the will of a family member:

"I direct that all bank accounts which stand in joint names with my attorney-in-fact, the executor of my will, and the successor trustee of my living trust, be used to pay for the expenses incurred in the settlement of my trust, and the remaining balance to be added to the residue of my pour-over will."

These instructions were inappropriate to include in the will because joint accounts are not will assets, but I did it anyway. The purpose was to inform the eight beneficiaries, when they read the will, that the testator desired that the accounts pay into the pour-over will, and hence into the trust. For that reason it was acceptable.

THE TRUST CHECKING ACCOUNT

Some lawyers advise against holding a checking account in your trust—specifically in your name as trustee of your living trust. They claim that when you sign your name on the check you will need to sign "(your name), trustee." What nonsense. Yes, if you sign your name and include "trustee", many clerks and cashiers at retail locations, where they know nothing about trusts, will refuse to accept or to cash your check.

If you want a trust checking account, there is no reason you can't have one. But your successor trustee probably won't need one. When it comes time for her to settle your trust, she can use your account on which she is a joint tenant.

The registration of your checking account is a private matter between you and the bank staff. No one else needs to know anything about your account. Even though the trust checking account belongs to you as trustee of your living trust, you don't have to advertise the fact. You can print your name and address on your checks just like everyone else does, and you don't have to write "trustee" after your signature.

— CHAPTER FOURTEEN —

TAXES

IT'S A SHAME, BUT ALMOST every decision we make in life has a tax consequence. What job to take, whether to start a business, where to live, what tax deductions are safe to take, which tax advisor is safe to hire, whether it is legal to open an offshore account to shelter wealth, and how to pass your estate to your loved ones free of taxes.

There are more than 55 federal, state and local taxes Americans have to pay. This is disgusting. If you want to see the complete list, make a Google search for "list of taxes we pay." A hundred years ago we had none of these taxes. And our nation was free of debt. Now we are a debtor nation with huge—and ever increasing—debt. This is debt we can never pay off.

Fortunately, creating a living trust, transferring assets into that trust, and thus developing a non-probate estate for yourself may reduce some taxes you will owe. The grantor must still pay taxes on income, earned and unearned. After the death of the grantor, the successor trustee must also pay taxes on income earned by the trust, but the computations can be done privately without submitting data to the probate court.

Fortunately, there are three taxes that we can do something about now, The Federal Estate Tax (Death Tax), The Gift Tax, and the Inheritance Tax (State Death Tax)

THE FEDERAL ESTATE TAX (DEATH TAX)

The Federal Estate Tax, also called the death tax, is a federal tax that Congress levied upon us, payable after our death, and before our wealth is transferred to our heirs and beneficiaries. If your estate is large enough you get taxed. Usually it's wealth you already paid tax on when you earned it. And the government decided to tax it again.

In 2018 the Federal Estate Tax threshold is $11.2 million, ($22.4 million for a married couple). If you die in 2018 your estate will owe tax on your net worth in excess of $11.2 million. The rate of taxation on the amount in excess of $11.2 million is 40 percent.

The desire to avoid tax is a reason trusts were created. And taxes are one of the reasons this book was written. Married couples with large estates, not knowing what the future holds, usually create an AB trust so that both spouses can take advantage of the estate tax exemption and thereby reduce death taxes. (The AB trust is discussed in Chapter 9).

If you have a large estate, or you anticipate increased earnings, or an inheritance that will put your estate above the exemption limit, I recommend you consider an AB trust and contact a tax attorney.

THE GIFT TAX

The tax law signed by president Trump on December 22, 2017 raised the Federal Gift Tax (the Generation Skipping Tax (GST)) lifetime exemption to $11.2 million and set the tax rate at 40%. That means you can gift $11.2 million in taxable gifts over your lifetime before owing any federal gift tax. What? Taxable gifts and no tax? That's an oxymoron. At the very least the Federal Gift Tax is a confusing law. I'll try to explain it.

You make a gift of money or property. The dollar amount of the gift is based on the value of the gift when you make it. When your cumulative lifetime gift total exceeds the lifetime gift tax exemption limit of $11.2 million (for those who die in 2018) a gift tax is imposed on the donor. The tax rate on the first dollar over the exemption limit is 40 %.

Wonderful, you give away $11.2 million with no tax. That sounds great, and you think that is a good deal. Well, maybe it's not such a good deal after all, because the total amount of your lifetime taxable gifts is deducted from the estate tax exemption allowed in the year of your death. For example, over your lifetime you have given away $9.2 million. You die in a year in which the gift tax exemption is $11.2 million. The $9.2 you gave away tax-free is deducted from $11.2 million gift tax exemption limit. As a result, your gift tax exemption is no longer $11.2 million. Your estate can pass only $2 million to you heirs tax free. Estate tax is due on the rest of your estate. The tax rate could be 40 %. Only conniving lawyers in Congress could come up with a deceptive scheme like this.

What did you gain with tax-free giving? Perhaps not very much. However, there is a better way to make gifts and still lower estate and gift taxes. It is the annual tax-exempt gift.

THE ANNUAL TAX-EXEMPT GIFT

In 2018 any person can give annually to any other person or non-charitable institution up to $15,000 tax-free. That is called the annual exclusion. It is a good deal. A married couple can give a combined gift of $30,000 annually tax free to any person or non-charitable institution. The amount does not have to come equally from each donor. One spouse can provide all the funds for the combined gift. If the couple has four children, and each child has a spouse, and there are six grandchildren, for example, the couple can give away, $30,000X14 = $420,000. If a couple is not married, they cannot give a split gift like this. Each would have to make individual gifts from his or her own funds, but that is easy. The outcome will be the same.

These $15,000 gifts can be made repeatedly each calendar year. The amount has been rising in recent years and may be increased in the future. What the amount will be in future years is yet to be determined; it depends on inflation. The amount can only be increased in increments of $1000. We hope everyone can afford this giving. It is easy, private, and tax free. No reporting is required

There is another way to help those in need. In addition to the annual exemption, any person can give any amount for someone's tuition payments and medical care (including medical insurance premiums). The payments must be made directly to the educational institution or medical care provider or insurance company. There is no limit to this amount, but the donor needs to pay the bills directly to the vendor. If the gift payments are made to the individual donee, the annual $15,000 exclusion limit will apply.

If you decide you want to give more than the annual gift exclusion of $15,000 to a person or non-charitable institution, you may do so. The amount of your gift in excess of $15,000 is taxable, but no tax is due until you exceed $11.2 million.

How are these taxable gifts tabulated? By using IRS Form 709, United States Gift (and Generation-Skipping Transfer) Tax Return. This is another complicated IRS Form. You should avoid it if you can. Also, filing an IRS Form 709 starts another paper trail with the IRS. It's better to remain private. You may want to consult a tax attorney before making taxable gifts.

INHERITANCE TAX (STATE DEATH TAX)

About a quarter of the states impose a state death tax. Most of these states impose no tax on inheritances received by spouses, parents, grandparents and children. But if the inheritance goes to others, the tax could be onerous. For example, a widow with no children plans to leave her estate to nieces and nephews. The tax rate could be 15 percent. The tax is imposed on the beneficiary. And the tax could start at the first dollar. For every $10,000 a niece or nephew is supposed to receive she or he could get only $8500, and the state gets $1500. Nice!

To find out if the state where you live imposes a death tax that will impact your estate, conduct a Google search for "(your state) death taxes." If you don't like what you see, there is a solution. If your state has death taxes that will treat you unfavorably, you can avoid the tax by establishing residence in a state that has no state death tax. You can find these states by searching Google for "states with no death tax". While you're at it, seven states (Alaska, Florida, Nevada, South Dakota, Texas, Washington, and Wyoming) have no state death tax or income tax. Thousands have already moved to those states to avoid taxes.

CHAPTER FIFTEEN

SOME IMPORTANT RECOMMENDATIONS

HERE ARE SOME IMPORTANT recommendations to help make probate avoidance a success and allow for easy settlement of your trust.

WHERE'S MY STUFF?

I recommend you start probate avoidance by making a list of all your possessions. It's a matter of getting organized. Compile a complete list of the assets you own, particularly the intangible personal property (the property with registration documents), the value of each, and the combined value. I hope you are pleasantly surprised with the total. This list will help you decide which type of living trust to create, a Basic Living Trust for the Individual, a Joint living Trust, an AB trust, or an AB Disclaimer trust, or perhaps several trusts. The list may help you decide what to give away now to reduce the size of your estate to stay below the estate tax threshold. Remember to subtract from the positive amount any negative balances such as the remaining balance on your existing mortgage, credit card balances, and other debts.

The list you create will be a table of contents of all your assets. What is it? Where is it located? How is it held (example: joint tenancy, individual ownership with P.O.D. designation, or held in a trust).

To see how your real estate is held, look at the deed. Look at the bank account monthly statement. If it's a joint account, is there a designated beneficiary? Perhaps you don't know. If the statement says John Doe (POD), who is the named beneficiary? You may have to call or make a visit to the bank to find out and make the changes you desire. Call the mutual fund company to ask how your mutual fund account is registered. While you're at it, ask them to send you the form so you can transfer the account to your living trust. Also ask for the form on which you designate a P.O.D. beneficiary (suggestion: your living trust). These forms may also be available on their website.

More than likely you will have to call your stockbroker too. Call or write all the financial institutions where the rest of your intangible personal property is held. Here is what is nice to know about each asset:

1. Type of asset.
2. The name and address of the business holding of the asset.
3. Phone numbers
4. Your account number.
5. Your member number if you are a member of a group.
6. Registration of the asset. (Example: joint, P.O.D., trust.
7. Name of account representative or best person to contact.
8. Contact person's phone number.
9. Web address. List the user ID, password, and PIN if necessary to access the account.
10. How are funds transferred in or out? Example: Electronic funds transfer from bank to broker and broker to bank. List routing numbers and account numbers.
11. When you call the bank, broker, insurance company or others, what are the questions they ask you to confirm your identity? What are the answers they have on file? List these questions and answers. (Your attorney-in-fact and successor trustees may need this information some day).
12. Where is the document for this asset stored?

On a separate piece of paper for each asset, list all the information about the asset. What type of asset, where it is located, address, phone numbers, and all the information suggested above. Add any extra information pertinent to each asset. There are at least two reasons for this: (1) All the data will be concentrated in one location. You can refer to the listing any time you need some information. You will be amazed how often you refer to this information, and (2) this information will be of enormous value to your attorney-in-fact and successor trustee if you become incapacitated or die.

Your collection of completed forms could be held in a loose-leaf notebook or in a computer file. As you add a new asset, add a new form to the collection. When the particulars of an asset change, make a new updated form. Keep this information secure. Tell you executor and successor trustee where the information is kept.

Now that you are organized and know everything about your "stuff", you can take action necessary to insure that each asset will avoid probate. (See Chapter 16 for the best ways to probate proof each asset).

DISTRIBUTION CONFUSION

People often create a confusing mess that complicates the final distribution of their assets. Here is an example:

Mel has four children. Soon after the birth of his first son, he bought a $25,000 whole life insurance policy. He named Son #1, Mel Jr. as the beneficiary. Son #2 was later named beneficiary of a savings account. The account value was usually in the area of $7,500. Mel received a $45,000 inheritance recently and bought a certificate of deposit. He listed his daughter #1, Lucille, as P.O.D. beneficiary of the CD. Mel lives in a state which permits Revocable Transfer-on-Death Deeds for real estate, so named his daughter #2 as T.O.D. beneficiary of his home just to keep it out of probate.

Mel created a large unintended disparity in the value of the property each child will receive upon his death. Confusing the issue is the fact that he specified in his last will that each child should receive equal shares of the estate. Mel created what I call **Distribution Confusion.**

We all know, or believe, that your Last Will and Testament is where you let everyone know what you want done with your possessions. And Mel did that. He specified that his four children should receive equal shares. Equal shares of what? What stuff? In reality, just equal shares of the stuff remaining in his will, and that's all. It excludes the assets that were removed from the will, namely all the assets for which there were designated beneficiaries. It also excludes any property that was held in a living trust, if Mel was smart enough to have created one.

Is your will up to date? Is your youngest child included? What if the distribution clause in your trust differs from the distribution clause in your will? Are you happy with the amounts each beneficiary is scheduled to receive? Is there a conflict?

Some of the beneficiaries may be unhappy with the amounts they receive. What are the executor and successor trustee to do? Distribute disproportional shares? Try to balance it out? Hold a beneficiaries meeting? Give up? It's a tough call.

Welcome to the world of **Distribution Confusion**. Distribution Confusion occurs in countless estates nationwide. It is a perplexing problem for the families and the executors. If you want to give disproportionate shares to the beneficiaries, that is your right. They should accept your reasons for doing so. In any event, you should prepare a non-probate estate that will permit easy trust settlement with no confusion about the final distribution of your assets. If the assignment of assets to beneficiaries conflicts with your larger distribution plan, you need to take action now to avoid Distribution Confusion.

The solution to Distribution Confusion is quite simple. Create your living trust first. Hold in your trust only those assets that need to be there. (See Chapter 16 for suggestions on what to hold in trust). Then name you living trust as P.O.D. or T.O.D. beneficiary for the intangible personal property. Make a pour-over will so that everything left in your will pours over into your living trust when you die. This way everything is collected in your trust and is distributed in accordance with the distribution instructions in the trust. If you want to give to a charity do it in your will or your trust, but not both unless you want a double gift to that charity.

Review your asset distribution plan with your executor and successor trustee. To eliminate conflict, the executor of your will and the successor trustee of your living trust should be the same person.

WHEN SHOULD YOU START PROBATE AVOIDANCE?

If you watched lawyers scurrying in and out of a dying client's bedroom as they desperately prepare a new will and a trust, you quickly realize that that client should have started probate avoidance long ago. If you are in your 60s and haven't yet started probate avoidance, it's time to get going. If you are in your 40s, it is very likely your parents are in their 60s, and if they haven't started probate avoidance, it's incumbent upon you to help them. Explain to them how much easier it will be for you and the rest of the kids if they probate-proof their estate. And explain the cost savings.

You can prepare your parents' living trust on the same afternoon you prepare you own. Age 40 isn't too young to get started. At age 40 you can expect to live for many more years, but, unfortunately, accidents do happen. So don't accept criticism for starting so young.

After the trust is created make a will and begin moving assets out of the will and into the trust. You don't have to spend full time on the project. You can establish your own time frame. One item at a time is sensible. Start with your home and other real estate. A lawyer can prepare a quitclaim deed to transfer all the real estate, or you can prepare the quitclaim deed yourself, have your signature notarized, and take the deed to the county Register of Deeds for recording. (A sample quit claim deed appears in the appendix). Prepare a new deed based on the property description in your existing deed.

Suppose you are in your 30s. Too young to have a living trust? Not at all. If you plan to buy a home, and you plan to be in that home for a few years, put the property in your trust. It is very simple, and easier than transferring the property to the trust later. Just tell the title company, bank, or lawyer who is preparing the title that you want to take title of the property as trustee of your living trust, and provide them with a copy of the Certificate of Trust

Over time you can probate proof all of your assets. It should be fun and very satisfying. Sure, lawyers tell you that probate doesn't happen until after your death, so it's not a big deal. Not for the lawyers it isn't. They stand to gain. They love to get hired to "fix the mess."

No matter your age, you can make probate avoidance a fun and satisfying experience. You will be doing something few others do. You are doing it for the children. Yes, you are. They will appreciate you thoughtfulness.

WHERE DO YOU STORE YOUR
LIVING TRUST AND YOUR WILL?

Attorneys frequently recommend that they store your trust and will in their vault for safekeeping. Forget that suggestion. That is not a good idea. You don't have easy access to your documents, and it provides the attorney with unreasonable favoritism for future employment to settle your estate when, in fact, your family could easily do it themselves.

When you create the living trust yourself and make your own pour-over will, an attorney won't be involved. When you do it yourself, there is little risk that your documents will end up in an attorney's vault.

The best place to store you documents is in a safe deposit box. Oh yes, attorneys recommend against storing your documents in a safe deposit box, since many states—particularly those states which love to search safe deposit boxes for stuff they can tax—restrict access to such boxes without probate court approval and a bureaucrat in attendance when your executor is allowed first entry. All this hassle is avoided if you store your documents in a safe deposit box leased by your trust. The trustee leases the box and pays the rent. After your demise your successor trustee can immediately enter the box. All that is required is his or her identification and a copy of the death certificate. The bank probably requested an Abstract of the Trust or a Certificate or Trust when you leased the box, so they should have that of file. If not, the successor trustee can provide that too.

Actions to Take:

Inventory your assets. Determine what type of trust you need—Individual, Joint, AB, or AB Disclaimer Trust. As you create a trust and make a new will, give generous thought to how to distribute your assets. Eliminate conflicts by changing beneficiary designations.

Age 40 is not too young to start probate avoidance. Help your parents with probate avoidance too. Explain to them how it will save the estate money and avoid a huge hassle for you and your siblings.

Store your living trust and your will in your safe deposit box. Tell the bank employee you wish to lease the box as trustee of your living trust. Provide the bank with a copy of the Certificate of Trust.

CHAPTER SIXTEEN

PROBATE AVOIDANCE FOR YOUR STUFF— ASSET BY ASSET

MOST ASSETS CAN BE PROTECTED from probate in several ways. Here is a look at each asset and the best method to probate-proof each considering paperwork, cost, and the ease with which the successor trustee can ultimately transfer the asset to the beneficiary.

SOLUTION 1: ASSETS BEST HELD IN YOUR TRUST

Let's start with the assets which should be held in your living trust. Because transferring assets to your trust usually involves more paperwork and expense than simply naming a P.O.D. or T.O.D. beneficiary, I suggest putting into your trust only those items which should be there. The list is short.

Be advised that the suggestions made here may differ from the recommendations made by some lawyers. That is one of the reasons you need to read this book. You get a second opinion. These second opinions will hold up extremely well under scrutiny.

REAL ESTATE

The best way to avoid probate for your real estate is to hold it in your living trust. That's indisputable. Why? Because when you sell real estate, the seller must prepare and sign a new deed in favor of the buyer. If the seller is deceased, the property goes through probate. However, if the property is held in a trust, the successor trustee can prepare and sign the new deed. No probate is needed. When you purchase real estate, tell the title company or lawyer preparing the deed that you want to take ownership as trustee(s) of your living trust. This is easy, and there is no extra cost.

Some lawyers suggest that if you buy real estate frequently with the intention of selling it soon, you don't need to hold it in your trust. Frankly, you don't know how long you might hold a property or when you will die. Why take a chance? Take title in the name of your trust. It's no extra work or extra cost and it's a safe way to insure that probate of that real estate is avoided.

It is very easy to transfer the real estate you currently own to your living trust. You must prepare and sign a new deed. A quitclaim deed is the most common devise. You can find blank quitclaim deed forms at office supply stores or on the web. The new quitclaim deed will state that you as owners, for example James and Robin Wheeler, of Anyplace, Kansas, joint tenants with right of survivorship, hereby quitclaim in favor of James and Robin Wheeler, co-trustees of the James and Robin Wheeler Joint Living Trust dated 9-12-1998, grantee, the following property _____.

The quitclaim deed is no more complicated than your existing deed. You can prepare it yourself or hire a lawyer to do it. (A sample quitclaim deed is included in the appendix). The quitclaim deed in the appendix was prepared for recording in a county that specifies a three-inch margin at the top of the page. That is the standard in many jurisdictions. It gives the county clerks room to apply their stamp. When you go to their office to record the new deed, it is fun to watch the bureaucrat use his ruler to check for three inches. A silly millimeter less and you end up paying an extra fee for nonstandard recording. It's usually a very small fee. I consider it a tax. You think this couldn't happen? It happened to me. The bureaucrat with ruler measured the margin at 3.015 inches. I was safe. It was hard to keep a straight face.

If you own a co-op apartment, you should transfer your share of the co-op to your living trust also. You will need to check with the co-op corporation to find out how this is done.

All the real estate you own in your county can be transferred to your living trust on the same quitclaim deed. You will need to prepare separate quitclaim deeds for real estate you own in other counties or states.

The deeds must be signed in front of a notary public, then taken or sent to the Register of Deeds office or county recorder's office in the county where the property is located. There will be a small recording fee. And, as noted above, an additional small charge if the deed is non-standard, i.e. doesn't conform to the county's peculiar format.

Transfer of real estate from yourself to yourself as trustee of your living trust is exempt from tax in most states. In some states such transfer could trigger a tax, but that should not discourage probate avoidance.

After you quitclaim real estate to yourself as trustee of your living trust, you should call your insurance company and advise them of the change. There should be no change in insurance premium.

When asked if you own your home you can respond with a great answer "it's in trust." This should impress about 15 percent of the populous who know a little about trusts, and confuse the other 85 percent who know nothing.

A Limited Alternative: The Revocable Transfer on Death Deed

Twelve states and the District of Columbia have passed laws allowing the transfer of real estate to a person you name as a death beneficiary without probate. The states are Arizona, Arkansas, Colorado, Kansas, Minnesota, Missouri, Montana, Nevada, New Mexico, Ohio, Oklahoma, and Wisconsin. The beneficiary is named on the deed. These Transfer-on-Death deeds must be signed, notarized and recorded at the county Register of Deeds office just like any deed. Unlike a regular deed, however, the transfer-on-death deed can be revoked. The deed should state that it does not take effect until death. If you are interested, check the statutes in your state.

Even though your state offers you a chance to name a beneficiary to receive your real estate, it doesn't help the rest of us who live in the remaining states. And it doesn't eliminate your need to create a living trust just so you can name your trust as the beneficiary of the Transfer-on-Death Deed (if that is allowed in your state), or as a P.O.D. beneficiary for a whole host of other assets. It's widely considered better to hold real estate in your trust.

Another Weak Alternative:
Adding a New Joint Owner to Your Deed

Adding the name of your son or daughter, or anyone for that matter, to the title of your real estate just to avoid probate is poor estate planning. That new person becomes half owner of the property. In most cases this handsome gift exceeds $15,000, the annual maximum tax-free gift limit. The gift may not be taxable immediately, but the gift amount is counted against the lifetime gift exclusion. In any event, the gift requires the filing of IRS Form 709, United States Gift (and Generation-Skipping Transfer) Tax Return. That's a complicated form. Most storefront tax preparers don't have a clue how to complete it. Most authors suggest using an attorney if you need to file the dreadful Form 709.

Here is another consideration: Which of your three or four children becomes half owner of the property to the exclusion of the others? How are you going to achieve equal or preferred giving to all the kids? (See Chapter 15, Distribution Confusion).

Recommendation: The living trust is the universally accepted best way to hold real estate. That includes agricultural land, co-ops, condos, duplexes, houses, marina dock space, mobile homes, rental property, residential lots, time-shares, and vacation homes. If you own real estate, you need a living trust.

VEHICLES

Most people do nothing to probate-proof their vehicles. As a result the vast majority of cars and trucks go through probate on the way to heirs and beneficiaries. Sure, in most states your car can be transferred to your heir as a probate exemption for small estates, but in many states the affidavit procedure allows vehicles to be passed to a new owner only if probate is not necessary for any of the deceased's other property. What executor or successor trustee deserves the hassle? Why rely on small estate procedures as part of your estate plan?

Fortunately, there are several ways to pass your car, truck, motorcycle, motor home, ATV, RVs, or other vehicles with title registration to your heirs or other beneficiaries without probate. Let's look at the options.

Register Your Vehicle In Your Name
As Trustee of Your Living Trust_

Many attorneys, even some widely read and respected estate planning attorneys, suggest that your car is better left to your heirs through your will and that living trusts don't work well for cars. That's bologna. They claim that insurance companies are reluctant to insure cars owned by trusts because the insurance companies can't tell who is authorized to transfer the car. What nonsense.

Let me explain it to the insurance companies right now. The trustee buys the car and titles it in his or her name as trustee of the trust. The trustee drives the car, refuels the car, and is responsible for maintenance. When it's time to sell the car, the trustee does that too. It's really not complicated. There is absolutely no reason not to hold your vehicles in your trust. It is without question the best way to keep your vehicles out of probate.

Thousands of cars are registered in the name of trusts. Insurance companies insure these cars because they want to increase market share and provide superior customer service. These companies understand the reasons for registration to a trust. They will be glad to accept your business. If the insurance company requests a copy of the trust, provide them with a sanitized copy or a Certificate of Trust. Then they will know the names of the grantor(s), the trustees, and the successor trustees, and the powers granted the trustees.

Titling your car or truck in your name as trustee of your living trust is not difficult. Someone at every DMV office will know how to do it.

Here is my true experience at a small DMV office shared with the county treasurer's office. I handed the clerk the titles to two antique cars which I have owned for a long time and intended to own forever. I asked that the cars be transferred to my trust. She gave me a blank stare and left. She went into conference with two other women in the back of the room. Then a man joined them. After the conference ended the three women came back to me. They explained that one of them knew how to transfer to a trust and the other two would watch and learn. The transfer went smoothly. The total cost was $10. This episode convinced me that transfer of vehicle to a trust is relatively rare at DMV offices. But it should be common.

A Limited Alternative:
Transfer-on-Death Registration for your Vehicles

So far, 14 states, Arizona, Arkansas, California, Connecticut, Delaware, Illinois, Indiana, Kansas, Missouri, Nebraska, Nevada, Ohio, Vermont, and Virginia allow some kind of transfer-on-death (T.O.D.) registration for vehicles. Other states may be adding this convenience in the future.

In some of these states you can hold title to your car, truck, motor home or other titled vehicles in joint ownership with someone else, your spouse for example, and name a beneficiary to receive the vehicle after the last registered owner dies. In the remainder of these states, T.O.D. registration is limited to one-owner vehicles and allows only one designated beneficiary, and you can't name a contingent beneficiary.

Whom should you designate as a beneficiary? It can be anyone you choose. The person doesn't have to be an adult or a licensed driver.

Preferably you should be able to designate a living trust as a transfer-on-death beneficiary. That would be a perfect choice. Sadly, in some of these states this is not permitted. The beneficiary has to be an individual.

You commonly name the beneficiary either on a title or application for title. In some states the beneficiary is listed on the registration. Of course, this is done at your friendly DMV office.

The designated beneficiary has no right to the vehicle until the last owner dies. The owner can change the name of a beneficiary or delete the beneficiary entirely by going to the DMV office and applying for a new certificate of ownership. Wow, another trip to the DMV. How frustrating!

After the death of the registered owner, the beneficiary must identify herself, present the certificate of ownership of the vehicle, present a copy of the death certificate of the deceased owner, and make application for a new certificate. The new owner inherits the vehicle and all outstanding debt. If there is a loan on the car, the beneficiary inherits the obligation to repay the loan.

Also remember, if you select the T.O.D. option, you will be giving the vehicle to one beneficiary at the possible exclusion of other beneficiaries. Is that really what you want to do? (See Distribution Confusion in Chapter 15).

If any of this excites those of you who live in these states, call your DMV office for more information. Frankly, why bother with the transfer-on-death option? It's easier to title the vehicle in your name as trustee of your living trust. And this option is available to everyone.

Two More Weak Options

1. Add the name of an additional owner to the title. If you are the sole owner of the car or truck, you can add the name of another person to the title. You will be creating a joint tenancy and will be giving the new owner a gift of half of the vehicle. If the value of the gift exceeds the annual tax-free gift amount—it probably won't unless this is

a valuable antique car—you may be required to file a gift tax return. When you die the surviving joint owner inherits the vehicle to the exclusion of the other beneficiaries. (See Distribution Confusion in Chapter 15).

2. Here is something else you can do. It is incredibly easy. On the back of most titles is a space where you sign your name when you sell the vehicle. Some folks suggest you sign the title now and let your executor find a buyer after your death and then fill in the buyer's name and other required data. I wouldn't hesitate to do this. No one will know when you signed your name. It is unlikely anyone will ever question the procedure. Some attorneys will tell you this is illegal, but they probably won't be able to tell you what law or statute is violated. Who cares?

Recommendation: The best procedure is to transfer the title of your vehicles to yourself as trustee of your living trust. If you are young and healthy, or plan to sell the vehicle soon, you may logically decide to leave the registration of your current vehicle as is but title the next vehicle to yourself as trustee of your living trust. Transfer of the titles of all your cars and trucks to your living trust should be easy at your DMV office.

PROCEDURES FOR YOUR AIRCRAFT AND BOATS

Airplanes and boats are not over-the-road or off-road vehicles, but they need probate avoidance procedures just like the rest of your vehicles. Holding these vehicles in your trust is recommended.

Aircraft: The Federal Aviation Administration registers all aircraft. I recommend you hold your aircraft in your trust. Forms are available at the FAA website, www.faa.gov. Download, complete, and submit form AC 8050-1. Some owners have reported difficulty in getting trust ownership for their aircraft through the FAA. As an alternative, form a corporation and register the aircraft to the corporation. And hold the corporation in your trust.

Large Boats: Large boats are registered with the US Coast Guard. Ownership forms are available at the Coast Guard website, www. uscg.mil. I recommend you hold your large boats in your trust.

Small Boats: Some states issue titles or registration documents for small boats. If you are issued a title or registration document for your small boat, I recommend you hold the boat in your living trust. Example: Ben Jones, TR U/D/T DTD 12-5-2006. (Ben Jones, trustee, under declaration of trust dated December 5, 2006).

BUSINESS INTERESTS

It is essential that you transfer your business interests to your living trust. Otherwise your business assets could someday go through probate. How you transfer the business interests depends on how the business is owned. But fear not—the transfer is easy and you can do it yourself.

Transferring your business interests to your living trust provides your successor trustee the authority to operate the business after your demise, hire someone to run the business if necessary, and ultimately sell the business. This can be done privately with no court involvement. Nonetheless, advice from an attorney concerning assignment of business property would be advisable.

Sole Proprietorships: If you are creating your living trust now, you can list your business by name as an item of property in your trust document. That transfers the business and the goodwill to the trust. Alternately, you can transfer the business and the goodwill, and all the business property and inventory, to the trust on an Assignment of Property document. The transfer is from your name as sole proprietor to yourself as trustee of your living trust.

There is no standard format for Assignment of Property, but you should list the business name, any fictitious firm names, doing-business-as filings, listing of trademarks and service marks, and description of tangible property. This document may ultimately constitute the best ownership papers the business ever had. Signing the assignment form before a notary is optional. (A sample Assignment of Property form appears in the appendix).

Trademarks and Service Marks: Even though you listed trademarks and service marks on the assignment of property form, you must also register ownership in the name of the trustee of your living trust. For instructions on how to accomplish this, go to the United States Patent and Trademark website, www.uspto.gov. From the homepage click on "Trademarks", and jump to "Assignments."

Solely Owned Corporations: If you own all the stock in a corporation, you need to cancel the existing stock certificate and issue a new one in your name as trustee. Follow the corporation's written procedures.

Closely Held Corporations: To transfer your shares in a closely held corporation to your trust, follow the corporation's by-laws and articles of incorporation. If transfers are forbidden for any reason, the by-laws will have to be changed to permit the transfer.

Partnership Interests: To transfer partnership interests, contact the other partners and modify the partnership agreement to show that your interest is now held in your living trust. If there is a problem or a conflict, see an attorney before you make any changes to the agreement.

Limited Liability Companies: You should get the consent of all the other owners before you can transfer your interest to yourself as trustee of your living trust. Usually it takes only a majority to agree, but it is better to have agreement of all. Google "(your state) LLC" for information. It is possible you can download the form necessary to request the transfer. Otherwise contact your state's Secretary of State for the form.

Limited Partnership: Contact the partnership's general manager to find out what paperwork is necessary to transfer your interest to your trust.

Copyrights: Attorneys recommended you hold your copyrights in your trust. You can transfer your existing copyrights to yourself as trustee of your trust with a copyrights assignment form. This form is available on your computer by searching Google for "copyright transfer form." The form should be filed with the U.S. Copyright Office. (See the U.S. Copyright Office website at www.uscopyright.gov for more help).

Patents: You should hold your patents in your trust. This can be done by using the sample assignment form in the appendix and recording it with the Patent and Trademark Office in Washington, DC. There is a small fee for the recording. See the U.S. Patent and Trademark website, www.uspto.gov for information.

All your patents can be included on the same assignment form. Signing the form in front of a notary is optional.

Royalties: If you receive royalty payments of any kind, your right to receive these payments can, and should, be transferred to your trust. This can be done with an Assignment of Property form (a sample can be found in the appendix) where you can definitively list the rights that you are transferring to the trust. You can give a copy of the assignment form to the company that makes the payments to you, but this is optional. In any event, after your death your successor trustee will take the necessary action to insure that the payments will forthwith go to your beneficiaries.

It is not necessary to sign the assignment form in front of a notary, but I recommend it.

Recommendations: All of your business interests should be held in your living trust. When you start or acquire a new business, place it in your trust. You should be able to make the transfers yourself or hire an attorney.

BROKERAGE ACCOUNTS

Most brokers permit designation of transfer-on-death beneficiary for brokerage accounts. But some do not offer T.O.D. designation for joint accounts. TD Ameritrade and Vanguard are two examples. If your broker does not offer T.O.D. designation for joint accounts, the account should be held in your living trust.

SAFE DEPOSIT BOXES

Some states, particularly those that have a state death tax, require that banks seal safe deposit boxes after the box holder dies. And the contents of the box cannot be released to anyone except the court appointed executor of the estate until a state bureaucrat arrives at the bank to "help" the executor open the box. This is done, of course, to allow the state to tax whatever he or she finds. The practice is obnoxious, offensive, and disgusting.

It happened to me in 1985 in Pennsylvania. After the bureaucrat arrived at the bank and directed the opening of my father's safe deposit box, she rifled the contents. She became interested in the title to a trailer. It was a homemade trailer that had years earlier become junk and been scrapped. I didn't enjoy having to convince her the trailer did not exist.

There is a better way to safeguard the box and its contents from the state. Transfer the box to your living trust. The trustee leases the box and pays the rent. Then you can safely store your trust, your will, all your private documents, and anything of value. If the grantor becomes incapacitated or dies, the successor trustee can enter the box to retrieve contents without interference. The bank knows how to set this up. They will probably ask for a copy of the Certificate of Trust. Provide them with one.

The other option is to authorize a family member or your successor trustee to enter the box at any time. The bank can easily set this up. The bank will need this person's signature on file.

SOLUTION 2: Avoid Probate with Pay-On-Death or Transfer-On-Death Designation

Many assets can be protected from probate by simply designating a pay-on-death beneficiary to receive the asset upon your death. This is very common and readily understood. And it requires no explanation to employees at the institutions where you have the assets.

BANK ACCOUNTS

Checking Accounts, Savings Accounts, and Money Market Accounts—in fact, all accounts, including jointly held accounts at a bank, savings and loan, credit union, or virtual online bank—may easily be protected from probate by designating these accounts pay-on-death to a beneficiary. Certificates of deposit (CDs) should also be designated P.O.D. This is the preferred method to avoid probate for bank assets. Naming your living trust as the P.O.D. beneficiary is a smart and sensible choice.

Agency Accounts that are professionally managed for clients by banks and trust companies can be held in your living trust if you wish, but it is easier to designate your trust as the P.O.D. beneficiary. Ask an officer of the institution to set it up for you. The paperwork should be simple.

Totten Trust Accounts are protected from probate. A Totten Trust is a special form of ownership that allows the account balance to pass automatically to a designated beneficiary upon the owner's death. The sole owner or joint owners register the account In-Trust-For the beneficiary. Typical wording would be: "Alice Smith, in Trust for James Smith, Jr."

The Totten trust resulted from a New York state ruling in 1904 which permitted a person to open a bank account as "trustee" for another person who had no rights to the assets until the depositor died. This opened the way for states to authorize pay-on-death accounts, sometimes called "informal trusts" or "bank trust accounts." Totten Trust accounts are still available today at some institutions.

If you go to your bank and ask to open a Totten Trust, you will probably receive a blank stare. Most bank employees won't have a clue as to what you are asking for. A supervisor or perhaps a lawyer working in the trust department will know, and will respond. "Oh, you want to open a P.O.D. account." Yes indeed, that is really what you asked for. None of these Totten accounts, whatever they are called, have an advantage over the universally available pay-on-death account.

Accounts Under Professional Management at a brokerage or investment company are not automatically protected from probate. Make sure the account is owned by your trust or is P.O.D. to the trustee of your trust. Either way will work. P.O.D. is probably easier and preferred. A short one-sentence letter should be sufficient to save you a personal visit. "Please designate my account number 1234567 P.O.D. to the trustee of the Dorothy Jones Living Trust dated 11-07-2004." A handwritten letter would be okay. Please try to write legibly and include a copy of the Certificate of Trust.

BROKERAGE ACCOUNTS

You can hold your brokerage account in your living trust. That is a one option. After your death your successor trustee takes over, sells the assets, and distributes the proceeds to the beneficiaries designated in your trust. This is done privately and free from probate. Alternately, you can name a beneficiary to receive your brokerage account after your death. That option is known as Transfer-On-Death (T.O.D.). There may be some legal difference between P.O.D. and T.O.D., but it makes no difference to the account owner. The account gets transferred to the person or trust you designate. The designated beneficiary gets the account without probate. In the meantime the beneficiary has no right to the account. You can name a new beneficiary, sell the stocks, or close the account any time you wish. You can impress you broker by asking for T.O.D. registration (rather than the more common P.O.D.). All brokerage firms have the forms necessary to create an account that is best for you.

Most states have adopted the Uniform TOD Security Registration Act, although some states have modified it. This is the law that permits T.O.D. registration of brokerage accounts. However, in many states brokerage firms may decide whether or not to offer T.O.D. registration. If your broker does not offer T.O.D., you can move your account to one that does or hold the account in your living trust.

T.O.D. should cost nothing to establish at most discount brokerage companies. Full service brokers are apt to charge a fee for opening the T.O.D. agreement, for changing it, and a processing fee when the account is transferred to the beneficiaries. Ask about your choices. There are some limitations with T.O.D. designation. In some cases you can name multiple beneficiaries but may not be permitted to designate alternate beneficiaries. If there is any problem with T.O.D. registration of persons as beneficiaries, then designate your living trust as T.O.D. beneficiary. There is a good reason for naming your trust as the T.O.D. beneficiary. The reason: your broker doesn't need to know the names of your final beneficiaries.

Some brokers do not offer T.O.D. beneficiary designation for joint accounts. Then you should hold the account in your living trust. This will prevent probate in case of simultaneous death of the joint owners.

SECURITIES

If you hold stock certificates or bonds in your possession—this is rare—there are several options. If these securities are registered, give them to a broker to be held in street name in your account. (Your account should be held in your trust or T.O.D. to your trust). Otherwise contact the transfer agent or company which issued the security and ask that the securities be reissued in your name as trustee of your living trust.

MUTUAL FUNDS

If you purchased mutual funds directly from the mutual fund company, contact the company and ask what is required to designate your account P.O.D. or T.O.D. to your trust. If the mutual fund company does not offer beneficiary designation for jointly owned accounts, then hold the account in your living trust. Ask for the forms to allow this transfer.

GOVERNMENT BONDS AND NOTES

You can register these instruments in beneficiary form as "payable on death to" a beneficiary as long as you purchase them as sole owner. The beneficiary must be a person; it cannot be a trust.

The government permits joint ownership with right of survivorship but no chance for naming a beneficiary. The bureaucrat who devised this system wasn't thinking or didn't know much about probate avoidance. He didn't take into consideration the fact that joint owners want to prevent probate in case of simultaneous death. And no one corrected this deficiency.

There is a remedy. Sole owners and joint owners should purchase the bonds in the name of their trust. For example, on the application joint owners would write "John Quincy Adams and Abigail Adams as co-trustees of the John Quincy Adams and Abigail Adams joint living trust dated November 4, 1805." As an alternate, you can use your own names, of course. Provide payment with the application. In about three weeks you will receive the bond in the mail, mailed to you from your distant but incredibly friendly Federal Reserve Bank. The bond will read "(your name(s) CO-TR U/D/T DTD 11-04-1805." Read that as "co-trustees under declaration of trust dated November 4, 1805."

After the death of the first owner (trustee), no action is necessary. Upon the death of the other trustee, the successor trustee takes the action dictated by the trust. The successor trustee can cash in the bond by presenting death certificates of all deceased owners, a copy of the trust or a certificate of trust, and his or her own personal identification.

If you already own EE or I Savings bonds and failed to name a beneficiary or wish to change a beneficiary, go to www.treasurydirect.gov and download the forms to reissue United States Savings Bonds. For EE savings bonds download PDF 4000, and for I Bonds download PDF 5387. Fill out the forms and mail them along with your bond to your local Federal Reserve Bank. In a few weeks you will have a new bond.

LIFE INSURANCE

Life insurance is purchased to provide for your spouse or family, to provide money to purchase your business partner's half of your shared business, or to pay estate taxes. These are just some of the reasons. Your selection of the beneficiary of the policy is an estate planning decision. It is advisable to get legal help when making these decisions.

Attorneys warn that life insurance proceeds are subject to probate if the beneficiary is your estate. ("your estate" means your probate estate). Choose a person as the beneficiary of life insurance. Or name a trust as beneficiary.

You can change the beneficiary designation of your life insurance policies at any time. Make sure the policies pay the beneficiaries you prefer.

RETIREMENT ACCOUNTS

Any money left in your IRA, Keogh, 401(k), or 403(b) accounts goes to the beneficiary you choose without going through probate. You do not pay income tax on the money you contribute to these plans, but Federal law requires mandatory withdrawal from 401(k)s and traditional IRAs. When your designated beneficiary withdraws money from these accounts, the tax deferral ends and the money is treated as the beneficiary's taxable income.

The rules for retirement plans are voluminous and complex. If you haven't already chosen a beneficiary for your existing accounts, ask the custodian of those accounts for rules that apply. Likewise for all accounts you open in the future.

Retirement plans are not will assets. They are distributed according to the beneficiary designation for each retirement plan. If you want a specific person to receive the plan after your death, you must designate that person. Married persons usually name their spouse as beneficiary for their plans, but someone else—children for example—can be named if your spouse agrees in writing. If you are not married, you can designate anyone you wish to receive the retirement plan after your death. In any event, if permitted, it is a good idea to name an alternate beneficiary to receive the plan. This eliminates the possibility that the account will become a probate asset in the event of simultaneous death of the plan owner and the only beneficiary.

Some retirement plans state that if you failed to designate a beneficiary or your named beneficiary is deceased, the plan will pass to your estate. Assets that pass into your estate ultimately go through probate. Make sure a beneficiary is named to receive the asset.

Some plans give a list of people to whom the plan will pay in order of priority (spouse, children, etc.). The list may not be the list you would prefer. Make sure you name the beneficiaries you prefer.

If you name your spouse as the beneficiary and then you divorce, she is automatically no longer the beneficiary, right? WRONG! Unless you change the beneficiary designation, your ex-wife gets the money. That should thrill your heirs. It is important that you keep the beneficiary designation up to date.

If you name your minor children as beneficiaries, they could get all the retirement plan funds when they reach the mature age of 18 or 21 depending on state law. But if you create a trust for the children and name the trust as beneficiary of the plan, the children will receive the plan proceeds in accordance with the dictates of the trust. That would be better.

Whom did you designate as beneficiary of your retirement plans? Do you remember? Did you even name a beneficiary? Better check with the custodian of the plan. And make the changes you wish, including alternate beneficiaries if allowed.

HEALTH SAVINGS ACCOUNTS

If you have a health savings account and haven't designated a beneficiary to receive the funds in the event of your death, contact the company that manages the account and ask how you can designate a beneficiary. Consider your living trust as first choice.

SUBSCRIBER ACCOUNTS

Some companies, particularly reciprocal (member owned) insurance companies, hold a portion of their capital in each member's name in a Subscriber's Account. The account is payable to the subscriber when he or she ceases being a member. When a member dies, the account becomes part of the deceased's estate. If you have a subscriber's or similar account, call the company to find out how your survivors can collect the money.

PAYPAL ACCOUNTS

The requirements for termination of a PayPal account are onerous. PayPal requires five documents from the executor. It is very burdensome. As an alternative, provide your executor or successor trustee with the username and password for the account. Then the funds can be easily withdrawn. Your checking account should be set up to receive transfers from PayPal.

FREQUENT FLYER MILES

Most airlines permit transfer of your frequent flyer miles to a beneficiary after your death. However, the airlines do not provide a method to designate that beneficiary on the application for their frequent flier program or permit you to list a beneficiary with the company. Some airlines allow transfer of miles to a new flyer at any time. Of course, your executor can do that for you after your death. He or she will need to know the account number, user names, and passwords.

Most airlines will transfer miles to a surviving spouse or even a family member with little fanfare. A common method is to send the airline a death certificate and a completed affidavit which the airline provides. Check with your airline to learn their specific procedure.

Frequent flyer miles are not the type of asset conveniently owned by your trust, so you should designate the beneficiary in your will. In the vast majority of cases you should be able to transfer the miles without involving the will, but having the beneficiary listed there is a backup plan.

SOLUTION 3: ASSETS TO LEAVE IN YOUR WILL

If They Ain't Broke, Don't Fix Them

In order to avoid probate I suggested you hold real estate, vehicle, business interests, and your safe deposit box in your trust. I then recommended naming beneficiaries to receive intangible personal property using Pay-on-Death and Transfer-on-Death designations. The other option—hold the intangible personal property in your trust. What's left? Tangible personal property, which are assets with no documentation. What do you do with them? Nothing. You leave them in your will. What are they? Here is a listing. It includes everything else you own. There are no registration documents with these items. Maybe a bill of sale, but that's all.

Animals	Furniture
Antiques	Furs
Art	Household Goods
Books	Jewelry
China, Crystal, Silver	Machinery
Coin Collections	Photo Equipment
Collectibles	Precious Metals
Computers	Stamp Collections
Electronic Equipment	Tools

Tangible personal property may be sold, traded, given away, or thrown away by you at any time. After your death your executor and successor trustee have those same options. If you made a pour-over will, these assets become trust property after your death and the successor trustee will be in charge.

Do nothing. Tangible personal property is a non-probate asset. Oh yes, you can transfer any or all of this stuff to your trust. Some people like to transfer the valuable items with an assignment of property document. If you think it is necessary or if it makes you feel better, then do it. Samples are in the appendix.

CHAPTER SEVENTEEN

HI KIDS:
A FATHER'S LETTER TO HIS CHILDREN

ED AND SHIRLEY JOHNSON LIVE in the small town of Upton, Wyoming. Ed was concerned because it took so long to settle the probate estate of a close friend and neighbor. And the cost was excessive. He didn't want that to happen to him.

Ed studied probate, what it entails, and what to do about it. He searched the literature for probate avoidance techniques. He was happily surprised to learn that anyone can probate-proof their estate, and can do it for very little cost. He also learned that attorneys rarely encourage anyone to do it themselves. So he set out to do it himself.

Ed ordered trust writing software and loaded it on his computer. He created the Edward and Shirley Johnson Joint Living Trust dated 7/20/12. It is a typical joint living trust used extensively by married couples. Edward and Shirley are the grantors. They are also the trustees and the beneficiaries of the trust. They named their son Edward Jr. as successor trustee and daughter, Stacy, as alternate successor trustee. Their children, Edward Jr., Stacy, and Carol are the final beneficiaries.

Ed and Shirley probate-proofed all of their assets. Recently they wrote a letter to the children explaining what they did. This is important. The kids need to know what they someday have to deal with. And they will be happy to know they can settle the estate (trust) privately, and no lawyers will be involved.

Everyone should write a letter of instructions. It is valuable information your successor trustees need to know. It will make their job a lot easier. **Note:** Upton is a town in eastern, Wyoming. The Johnson family is fictitious.

Dear Ed, Stacy, and Carol,

Shirley and I created a joint living trust and probate-proofed our estate. We did it privately without a lawyer.

We have three real properties: our home at 801 2ND Street in Upton, Shirley's floral shop in Upton, and a vacant lot in Scottsbluff, NE. We were joint tenants on the deeds for these properties. We prepared a single quitclaim deed for the Upton properties, quitclaiming the properties from ourselves as joint tenants, to ourselves as trustees of the Edward and Shirley Joint Living Trust dated 7/20/12. We had our signatures notarized, and recorded the deed at the Register of Deeds office in the county courthouse.

The Scottsbluff property needed to be transferred to the trust too. Failure to do so would result in ancillary probate in Nebraska. We created a quitclaim deed for that property, had our signatures notarized, and sent the deed with payment by mail to the Register of Deeds in Scotts Bluff County, Nebraska. That was another easy project.

All deeds were returned to us by mail with the proper county seal affixed. When it is time to sell any of these real properties, you will, as trustees of the living trust, prepare and sign a new warranty deed transferring the properties to the buyer without probate. You can prepare the warranty deed yourself or have an attorney do it.

We have two cars and an old pickup. We took the titles to the DMV office had the titles transferred to the trust. This isn't done often, but there was a woman in that office who knew how to do it. The fee was very reasonable. The new titles

(CONTINUED ON NEXT PAGE)

came in the mail from the state capitol. When it is time for you to sell these vehicles sign the back of the titles with (your name), trustee.

Aircraft need to be held in a trust. Shirley and I have had a lot of fun flying the Piper Tri-Pacer. We went to the FAA website, faa.gov, and downloaded FAA form AC 8050-1, Aircraft Registration Application. It was difficult getting the application accepted but we were eventually successful. The Tri-Pacer is now held in the trust.

Shirley's floral business is held in the trust. The business is registered with the state of Wyoming as a Wyoming LLC. We transferred the business and the goodwill to the trust on an Assignment of Property document. The document is in the safe deposit box in the Farmers and Merchants Bank. You will ultimately serve as trustee of the trust and can operate the business until you find a buyer.

My patent for the semi automatic semi adjustable multi-clamp is held in the trust. The patent certificate is in the safe deposit box.

The right to the royalty payment for the manufacture and sale of the semi automatic semi adjustable multi-clamp has been assigned to the trust by an Assignment of Property letter. The payer is aware of the assignment and makes payment to the trustees of the trust.

We have a joint brokerage account with Vanguard. They do not offer T.O.D. beneficiary designation for joint accounts. The Vanguard account in joint ownership becomes a probate asset if the owners suffer simultaneous deaths. So we hold our account in the name of our living trust.

TD Ameritrade also fails to offer T.O.D. beneficiary designation for joint owners. Our TD Ameritrade account is

(CONTINUED ON NEXT PAGE)

(CONTINUED)

held in the trust.

The safe deposit box at the Farmers and Merchants bank is registered as being held (leased) by the trustees of the trust. When we are gone you will serve as the new trustees and may enter the box.

The checking account, a savings account, and a certificate of deposit at the Farmers and Merchants Bank are designated pay-on-death (P.O.D.) to the living trust. This was very easy to do. All banks will add a beneficiary or change the beneficiary designation upon request. It is much easier than transferring the asset to the trust. Since you (Ed Jr. and Stacy) are also joint tenants on the checking account either of you can use this account as a convenience checking account if we ever need assistance managing the account and paying bills. In the meantime we will continue to use it as our everyday account.

Shirley has an account at the Upton Federal Credit Union. Our living trust is the P.O.D. beneficiary.

We have a brokerage account with Edward Jones Investments. They offer T.O.D. beneficiary designation for joint accounts. The living trust is the T.O.D. beneficiary.

Our life insurance, retirement accounts, and health savings accounts all have designated beneficiaries.

We have a small PayPal account. Use our username and password to access the account and electronically move the money from PayPal to our account at Farmers and Merchants Bank. The username and password are in the safe deposit box.

Everything listed above has a deed, title, or registration document. Everything else below is a will asset.

All of our tangible personal property is will property. Shirley and I have written holographic wills that are accept-

(CONTINUED ON NEXT PAGE)

ed in Wyoming. These are pour-over wills. All will assets pour over into the trust.

Furniture, tools, hobby items, farm equipment, books, paintings, and household furnishings can be keep, given away, sold, or thrown away. Take what you want and dispose of the rest.

On your next visit we will discuss everything in this letter and answer all questions.

Love,
Ed and Shirley

APPENDIX

PREPARED BY:
Ed Johnson
801 2nd St.
Upton, WY 82730
Ph: 307-782-XXXX

QUITCLAIM DEED

Edward and Shirley Johnson, of Upton, Wyoming, joint tenants with the right of survivorship, as Grantors, do hereby convey and quitclaim to Edward and Shirley Johnson, trustees of the Edward and Shirley Johnson Joint Living Trust, dated July 20, 2012, the Grantee, the following real properties located in Weston County, Wyoming to wit:

In the city of Upton, WY, **LOT 11, BLOCK 8 CLARKE AND BENSON'S ADDITION,** being a subdivision of Tract A of the NW1/4NE1/4 of Section 12 Township 6 South Range 2 East, Black Thunder Meridian, as set out in Weston County Plat Document 16-3916. The address is 801 2nd St. Upton, WY.

In the city of Upton, WY, **LOT 4, BLOCK 6 CLARKE AND BENSON'S ADDITION**, being a subdivision of Tract A of the NW1/4NE1/4 of Section 12 Township 6 South Range 2 East, Black Thunder Meridian, as set out in Weston County Plat Document 16-3916. The address is 301 Main St., Upton, WY

TO HAVE AND TO HOLD the said premises, with their appurtenances unto the said Grantee, and its assigns forever. And the said Grantor does hereby covenant to and with the said

(CONTINUED ON NEXT PAGE)

(CONTINUED)

Grantee, that they are the owners in fee simple of said premises; that they are free from all encumbrances except rights-of-way, federal patents and mineral reservations, easements, and building and use restrictions of record, and that they will warrant and defend the same from all lawful claims whatsoever.

This Quitclaim Deed is dated this _____th day of July, 20XX

_____   _____
Edward Johnson, Grantor   Shirley Johnson, Grantor

STATE OF WYOMING)

                ): ss.

County of WESTON   )

      On this _____th day of May, 20XX, before me, a Notary Public in and for the said State, personally appeared EDWARD JOHNSON and SHIRLEY JOHNSON, known to me to be the persons whose names are subscribed to the within instrument and acknowledged to me that they executed the same.

_____

Notary Public for the State of Wyoming
Residing at _____, Wyoming
My Commission Expires_____

LETTER OF ASSIGNMENT

Shirley Johnson Letter of Assignment

301 Main St.
Upton, WY

WITNESSETH, that for valuable consideration in hand, receipt is hereby acknowledged by the Assignee to the Assignor. The Assignor, Shirley Johnson, sole registered agent of the Shirley's Floral Shop LLC, a State of Wyoming Limited Liability Company (UBI Number 603-XXX7-XXX) hereby assigns the Shirley's Floral Shop LLC and all rights, and all of the assets of the LLC, to Edward and Shirley Johnson, trustees of the Edward and Shirley Johnson Joint Living Trust dated July 20, 2012, the Assignee.

IN WITNESS THEREOF, the Assignor has executed this assignment on the ____th day of_____, 20XX

Assignor: _____
                    Shirley Johnson

Assignee: _____   _____
                    Edward Johnson, trustee   and   Shirley Johnson, trustee

(CONTINUED ON NEXT PAGE)

STATE OF WYOMING)

): ss.

County of Weston)

On this _____ th day of _____, 20___ before me, a Notary Public in and for the said State, personally appeared Edward Johnson and Shirley Johnson, known to me to be the persons whose names are subscribed to within this instrument and acknowledged to me that they executed the same.

_____

Notary Public for the State of Wyoming

Residing at_____, Wyoming

My commission expires _____

LETTER OF ASSIGNMENT

Witnesseth, that for valuable consideration in hand, receipt is hereby acknowledged by the Assignee to the Assignor. The Assignor, Edward Johnson, of Upton, Wyoming, sole owner of U.S. Patent Number 123456789, Semi-adjustable Multi Clamp, hereby assigns Patent Number 123456789 to Edward Johnson and Shirley Johnson, trustees of the Edward Johnson and Shirley Johnson JT LV TR DTD 7-20-2012, the Assignee.

IN WITNESS THEREOF, the Assignor has executed this assignment on the _____th day of_____, 20__

Assignor: _____
                    Edward Johnson

Assignee: _____   _____
                    Edward Johnson, trustee   and   Shirley Johnson, trustee

STATE OF WYOMING)

                                    ): ss.
County of Weston   )

   On this _____ th day of _____, 20__ before me, a Notary Public in and for the said State, personally appeared Edward Johnson Shirley Johnson, known to me to be the persons whose names are subscribed to within this instrument and acknowledged to me that they executed the same.

_____
Notary Public for the State of Wyoming

Residing at_____, Wyoming

My commission expires _____

HOLOGRAPHIC WILL

Approximately half of the states honor holographic wills. Below is my South Dakota holographic will.

Holographic Last Will and Testament

I Sam Hauck, of Spearfish, South Dakota, on this date of February 28, 2012, make this holographic will. I am of sound body and mind and capable of determining my affairs.

I make this will in my own handwriting. I request the Court accept this as my handwritten holographis Last Will and Testament

This will superdedes all my previous wills and codicils.

From time to time I may attach to this will a list of tangible personal property items in my will that I wish to bequeath to specific individuals or entities. All personal property not so bequeathed shall pour-over into the Sam Hauck living trust dated 5/20/10.

Signed this 28th of February 2012 in Spearf sh, SD
Signed   Sam Hauck

THE FIVE IMPORTANT DOCUMENTS

There are five important documents everyone needs to probate-proof their estate and provide for management of their affairs.

1. The Declaration of Trust — This is the Revocable Living Trust document. When properly prepared and funded, it protects from probate those assets held in the trust, and it serves as a pay-on-death beneficiary for a wide range of other assets. The trust permits successor trustee supervision of your trust assets if you become incapacitated. A Certificate of Trust (or Abstract of Trust) is a shortened version of the trust you can give to banks, brokerage firms and others who ask for a copy of the trust. It certifies that the trust exists, names the grantors, the trustees, and the powers of the trustees. It does not include confidential information such as the names of the beneficiaries or how the trust assets are to be distributed. Most living trust packages will provide this document. However, It is not absolutely necessary that you have this document, and you should not have to pay more to get it. As an alternative you can prepare a "sanitized" copy of the original trust yourself by blanking out the confidential information, and providing sanitized copies to those who request it.

2. A Last Will and Testament — Specifies who get the assets in your will. The Pour-Over Will specifies that the assets in your will shall be transferred to your living trust after you die, so they can be distributed as part of your trust assets.

3. Durable Power of Attorney — When you give a trusted person power of attorney, he or she is authorized to handle your affairs. This person, known as an Attorney-in-Fact, can handle financial affairs, and prepare and sign tax returns. This power remains effective even if you become

incapacitated. It terminates upon the death of the person granting the power.

4. Living Will — Lets your physician know the kind of life support treatment you want in case of terminal illness or injury.

5. Durable Power of Attorney for Health Care — Lets you give legal authority to another person to make health care decisions for you if you are unable to make them for yourself.

TEN THINGS YOUR LAWYER WON'T TELL YOU

1. I am a general practitioner. I don't know much (or care) about total probate avoidance.
2. I really don't specialize in trusts or other probate avoidance techniques.
3. My estate clients end up in probate anyway and need a lawyer.
4. Avoiding probate is really simple and costs almost nothing. You can easily do it yourself.
5. You should have a living trust in additional to a will.
6. I could create living trust for you, but I would rather write a will for you now and do the probate later.
7. As executor you can settle the estate yourself and save big bucks.
8. You don't really need me.
9. I hand off work to peons but charge you a lawyer's rate.
10. Did you check on me before coming to me for help?

INDEX